IT'S A SIN
TO BORE A KID

IT'S A SIN TO BORE A KID

THE STORY OF YOUNG LIFE

CHAR MEREDITH

WORD BOOKS
PUBLISHER
WACO, TEXAS

ISBN 0-8499-0043-3
Library of Congress catalog card number: 77-83312
Printed in the United States of America

To
Maxine Rayburn
a renegade saint who persevered

Foreword

THE PURPOSE of this book is not simply to recall happy events or expose hurtful episodes in the minds of those who have lived the story. It is written for a much broader purpose: to celebrate the sovereign hand of God which we have personally witnessed over the years. Here you will view a small corner of the mosaic of God, one which nevertheless fits into this overall design. We felt telling it would be an encouragement to others at work in the Kingdom in our time. We hope that looking back over the trail we have left may also help us recognize future directions God desires us to take in Young Life.

More than five years have passed in the preparation of this book. Many times we have puzzled over why it took so long to get the manuscript into publishable form. We have been over-whelmed with the amount of material available. With each clue Char Meredith would track down, she'd find another beautiful account of God's entering a human life to make it fully alive. The plot divided and multiplied across the world. Thirty thousand miles of travel netted dozens of in-depth interviews with board members, staff, and club kids. The Rayburn family gave countless hours, unlocking their secret hearts as well as thirty-five years of Jim's personal files and journals. We are grateful to all those who spoke frankly, with laughter or with tears.

God chose a relative outsider to grasp the significant elements of how he was working out his purpose through this innovative band of disciples. Here was one who had not been as close as the rest of us, for as long a time—one who, not being identified with any single aspect of the mission, could see God moving throughout all aspects. While Char had spent several years articulating and interpreting the thrust of Young Life, she now had gotten into our roots more deeply than anyone ever had. The sifting process was slow and difficult. The filter of time was essential. Allowing the original input to settle, to be shuttled about by numerous qualified people, electrified us with a panoramic view of the unmistakable hand of God on our efforts.

Char's earliest title for the book was *In Spite Of Us*. That is the truth which burst from hours of listening. "In spite of" the people who lived this American epic—good people, intelligent, creative, visionary, stumbling people—God emerges the hero. "In spite of" all we have done to louse up the design, God has stepped in at the various junctures and led us correctly. Which is just what he has done again during the completion of this manuscript. Once again we have changed leadership.

During my thirteen years in the office of president I have often wondered when it would be time for me to step aside. Recently we have again witnessed the uncanny leading of God as the need for a change in leadership style has been called for by many.

Bob Mitchell, who as a Dallas high school student, met the Savior in one of Rayburn's early campaigns, is well suited to lead the ongoing ministry of Young Life. My thirty years of working side by side with Mitch has given me a great admiration for this gifted man of God, and I love him as a brother. Again God has intervened, imposing his sovereign desire and choosing his own instrument. What he is teaching us about following him is the supreme essence of living. God has enabled the tangled roots of our history to be pulled together with an overall clarity that is awesome. Read it carefully. It is an up-to-date record of God's sovereign movement among men.

BILL STARR

8

1

IT WAS AN ordinary residential street after dinner. A gray-haired man in a jumpsuit knelt at the sidewalk, setting out striped petunias. A little girl chased a black kitten up the tree in the next yard. Coming slowly around the corner was a Good Humor truck. Ding-ding. Ding-ding. Ding-ding.

A car pulled up to the curb across from the petunias, and eight kids tumbled out all the doors. A van honked and turned into the driveway. Two girls from the first car raced over to catch a pile of pillows and a bulging cloth bag the driver tossed at them. A guitar protruded from the van's back door as a voice bellowed out, "Day-O, Da-a-ay-O!" A motorcycle careened into the driveway, and a long-haired girl jumped off the back and threw her arms around the guitar player. Two more cars stopped in the middle of the street and kids piled out. One of them screeched up to the corner, then turned around and came back. The other took off. Two guys wrestled on the lawn. A couple of girls on the steps cheered, then returned to talking about the books they held.

Within a few minutes after the first car arrived, the front yard was thickly planted with high school kids. There was a shrill whistle, and the front door opened. The man in the jumpsuit stood up in time to see seventy-two kids disappear into his neighbor's house. Laughter erupted from the windows, accompanying a clown in complete makeup, who whooped down the stairs and around the side of the house. As Mr. Jumpsuit plopped

9

the last petunia into the sandy soil, he heard the guitar again and the mounting sound of two-part harmony, with hand-clapping on the beat. As he walked down the driveway, he tried to catch the words: "Then one day I met him face to face (ah-ah-ah-ah), and I felt the wonder of his grace (ah-ah-ah-ah), and I knew that he was more than just a God who didn't care, who lived a-way-out-there, and, now he walks beside me day by day, ever watching o'er me lest I stray, helping me to find the narrow way. . . . He's everything to me!"

Then it was silent. "What in thunder are those kids doin' over there at the Bergstroms?"

An hour later he looked up from his newspaper as the Bergstroms' front door flew open and the seventy-two kids poured back out, almost like a movie on rewind. Those who came in the van climbed back in. The driver who hadn't stayed drove up to collect his passengers. He heard a girl cry out, "Oh, Steve, you missed it tonight." The motorcycle growled and then roared away with Miss Long Hair astride the back, her arms hooked around Boy Friend. The bicycler stood for a moment to talk with another couple sitting on the hood of the car that was left. As the door slammed on the last goodbye, the kids slid off the hood, and the driver swung into the van and drove down the street.

Mr. Jumpsuit stared into the twilight. There was nobody left. The black kitten sat in the driveway as the little girl next door called, "Kitty, kitty." He turned back to his newspaper to see a headline about the teenager in the next suburb who had put a bullet through his brain. "Kids!" he muttered. "If I didn't see it with my own eyes, I wouldn't believe it."

That was Young Life Club night in Clinton. The guy in the van was the leader of the club. And the kids were there for the most part because he was their friend, but also because they liked being where other kids are. The clown had conducted a pudding-eating contest, of all things, which Mr. Jumpsuit might have found a bit messy. Three couples were picked to lie on the floor, head-to-head, and feed each other. The "winners," who cleaned out the pudding dish first, got to collect the song books in the cloth bag at the end of the meeting.

The music came out of well-worn, paperback, no-note song books, with the club leader and the guitar player shouting out the numbers. When all became quiet, the leader stood up with a book in his hand. It would have surprised Mr. Jumpsuit to know it was a Bible. With those wild kids? Why?

Because he believes that people are created to live life as fully as possible and that the Bible is made up of principles that actually do make life work better. The leader had started out by telling the kids how scared he was the first time he parachuted from an airplane. And he ended up telling them about a successful tax collector named Levi, A.D. 30, who turned his back on his drive-in vault and his four-speed camel to follow an itinerant preacher named Jesus.

In a relaxed home setting, sitting on the floor with their friends, these kids let their world come to a standstill as they ponder this Jesus who could turn grown men around and start them on a totally new track. In the process of that club meeting, and 1100 others like them across the United States, something new and alive brushes the consciousness of a girl here, a boy there. A sense of discovery grows, as perhaps for the first time a kid senses that God is real, that He is knowable. The creator of the universe is so personal that He is interested in the plainest or zaniest high school kid, and He is so big He is seeking a relationship with all kids everywhere.

The club is the platform of Young Life, but it's not the beginning. Young Life starts when a leader forms a friendship with a kid. Leaders go where kids are, spend hours wherever they come together. These friendships give leaders the opportunity to earn the right to be heard. Out of small talk after football practice or at a rock concert or the local McDonald's comes the right to share in the hurts and the happiness of these new friends. The kids like finding someone older who is just like them but who knows a lot more about life. Then at clubs throughout the school year, the leader is able to share his deepest beliefs about what makes life good for him—a life lived in relationship with Jesus Christ.

In 1977, Young Life clubs in the United States, Canada, and other countries had 70,000 teenagers in attendance each week.

11

More than 200,000 kids had significant contact with Young Life during the year. And 600 full-time staff were assisted by 200 part-timers and 6,000 volunteers to keep the clubs going.

All this began with one rebel who could not fit into the religious system of the '30s. He was Jim Rayburn. His story—as well as the story of Maxine, the woman he married, and of his colleagues—constitutes an extraordinary record of God's moving in the affairs of ordinary people.

2

IT WAS A cold winter night when Jim Rayburn spotted Maxine Stanley in a church balcony and introduced himself. She was seventeen, and he was not yet twenty. To be together, they enrolled at Kansas State College, where Jim studied civil engineering and Maxine became a freshman beauty queen. For two years, they were inseparable. Then in 1932, they headed to a justice of the peace to be married. Maxine later told friends, "Jim's folks had a fit and made us get married again three months later in a religious ceremony. Jim thought it might pacify them. I thought it kind of a farce. But I was willing to do anything to win his folks over. I think they regarded me as some kind of heathen. There had never been much religion in my home."

Jim's father was a Presbyterian evangelist who traveled from town to town preaching wherever he could pitch his tent. Jim went with him, often playing the cornet and leading a choir. Every night he heard about the evils of drinking, card-playing, dancing, and gambling. Even after he and Maxine were married, Jim had to return to his father's evangelistic team to make a living. He didn't like it much, but it offered him a job of sorts at a time when employment was at its worst and nobody was hiring engineers.

Jim and Maxine

Living with Jim's parents during that time offered a questionable kind of security to Maxine. Her parents had divorced when she was three. By the time she was thirteen, she had learned to run away. When things got too bad, she made a habit of removing herself. If she really wanted to do something, she could scheme and plan and find a way. Now what she wanted more than anything else was to be with her husband.

One night a man from the Presbyterian Board of National Missions came into the Rayburn tent and asked Jim if he would consider a job as a Presbyterian lay preacher. He would be visiting small communities throughout the Southwest. Was it the kind of job to which he could bring his wife? Yes. And would there be a salary sufficient to support them? Yes. That was all Jim had to hear. He leaped at the chance, even though he had no training for the job.

Carrying the message of Christ from town to town took Maxine and Jim on long automobile trips crisscrossing New Mexico and Arizona. Life was very full, very happy, and they were very poor. Their hours were full of searching and finding. Ordinary life did not attract them. They loved the desert vastness, its growth and its risks. They sought the high moments; but in the finding they began to sense that the heights were not necessarily the same for Maxine as they were for Jim.

He preached in one-room churches, in schoolhouses, under trees. As far as Jim was concerned, God's territory was everywhere. Most of his sermons were adaptations of those he had heard his father preach, but Jim's somehow came out happier. He talked more about the joy to be found in turning to Jesus

and less about sin. "Always," Maxine said, "he saw life as a great adventure." Jim enjoyed the work beyond all his expectations.

Wherever he went he'd stop the car and go over and pass the time of day with two or three kids. Young, informal, cheerful, he didn't look at all like a preacher. Maybe he'd talk about the school in town, or the baseball team, or some of the crazy things he'd seen kids do in other places. He liked to make them laugh. Teenagers were special to him long before they became the prize of the commercial marketplace. They were open, direct. They weren't uptight about a lot of things. It seemed a fertile age to learn and grow.

Jim was a great kid at heart. It was natural for him to be with kids and do things they liked to do. He and Maxine took them off to camp where they lived in crude cabins or well-worn tents borrowed from the Boy Scouts. They took teenagers on hikes and mountain climbs, sat with them around campfires, and talked about all sorts of things. Coming up with new ideas to attract kids kept the Rayburns praying and preparing. Jim built a chalk-talk easel for Maxine. Youth choirs worked in some places. A little mimeographed newspaper was circulated between villages. Every move was made to be closer to kids.

But what about the next step? How could he lead these boys and girls into an acceptance of Christ? How could he answer the strange, searching questions they asked?

During the early '30s, Jim's own active rebellion against traditional religious structures laid the foundation for his effectiveness with kids. Once, after attending a Presbyterian Synod, he wrote in his journal, "It was a perfect bore. Sat through the whole thing and shall regret it the rest of my life." He began to wonder how much he was missing of the significant meanings of the gospel. He began to realize how far he was from being an authority on matters in the Scripture. To deal in superficial clichés was not his way of satisfying his own hunger, or the doubts of his young friends. To him it was a sin to bore kids with the gospel.

Running through the warm spirit of adventure which Jim shared with the kids was an uncomfortable hard line left over from his family heritage. Most of what he was preaching on Christian living was a replay of the cultural taboos he had heard all his life. Maxine puzzled over the contradiction she felt: "Jim and I used to have such good times dancing at the university. What's the matter with him?"

One night in Clifton, Arizona, where they had moved into a decrepit old manse, Jim uncovered a secret that would change his life. Maxine had gone to a movie because she was tired of not doing anything that was fun by her standards. When she came home, Jim was so excited that he sat her right down and read to her from a dusty old book. He had found it on a shelf in the library. It was beat-up and coverless, but it contained ideas that kept them talking for two weeks. It was written by Lewis Sperry Chafer, president of a seminary in Dallas. And the title was simply *He That Is Spiritual*.

By the time they reached page 82, they knew they were on a new journey. Here Chafer talked about "grace truth." For the Rayburns it opened locked doors. "True spirituality is a divine output of the life, rather than a mere cessation of the things which are called 'worldly.' It does not consist in what one does not do; it is rather what one does. It is not suppression; it is expression. It is not holding in self; it is living out Christ. Worldly Christians turn to so-called worldly things because they discover in them an anesthetic to deaden the pain of an empty heart and life. . . . The cure is to fill the heart and life with the eternal blessings of God. . . . A dead leaf that may cling to the twig through the external raging storms of Winter, will silently fall to the ground when the new flow of sap from within has begun in the Spring. A dead leaf cannot remain where a new bud is springing, nor can worldliness remain where the blessings of the Spirit are flowing. We are not called upon to preach against 'dead leaves.' We have a message of the imperishable Spring. It is the outflow of the limitless life of God."

Added to the openness Jim loved in teenagers, this insight into the pain and the cure completed the outline of a clear call. What greater utilization of life than the filling of empty hearts and minds with the limitless life of God!

"Somewhere along the line," Maxine observed, looking back to that night in Clifton, "God sees a certain thing he wants done at a certain time, and he chooses a certain person to do it."

Jim's next step was to explore where he should go back to school. His application to Princeton Theological Seminary was refused because his engineering training was not appropriate. What the Rayburns did then was to cram all their possessions into the old Chevy and set off, not knowing where God wanted them. A few miles out of Clifton, they stopped at the highway going east and west. To the west was San Anselmo, a Presbyterian seminary in California. To the east was Dallas Theological Seminary in Texas. If Jim went to San Anselmo, the Presbyterians would almost certainly guarantee him a job. At Dallas, they would be on their own. "Which way shall we go, hon?"

"I think we should go east." Maxine knew that in Jim's deepest heart he longed to be able to study face to face with the wise and gracious man who had spoken to them the "message of the imperishable Spring." After considering briefly the benefits of both, and a few moments of prayer, Jim turned the car toward Dallas and Lewis Sperry Chafer.

3

IN THE LATE '30s, a power-crazed Hitler was launching invasions in Europe. His troops had blasted their way into the Rhineland, Poland, Austria, in his quest for world domination. Within a few brief years, they would embroil the United States in the most awesome war in history. The teenagers would become the fighting soldiers of that war, and 1,078,163 of them would become its casualties, dead or maimed. But were any of them fearing such things? Not much, outwardly.

What did worry them was the difficulty of finding work for the summer, and the more remote concern of the job problems they would have to face after high school graduation. Even more disturbing was the spectacle of their fathers looking in vain for work.

Young people found countless and zany distractions. A few ridiculous boys were swallowing live goldfish. Some were perching atop flagpoles. Others were setting records for the number of people who could squeeze into a telephone booth. Such things, nonsensical as they were, brought escape from the gloom of war that hung over their heads.

And what about religion? Were teenagers giving much attention to preachers? Were they finding strong guidance in the pulpit? One had to doubt that. It was more fun to listen to radio's Amos 'n' Andy, Edgar Bergen and Charlie McCarthy, Fred Allen, and Jack Benny. For sheer kicks hymns could hardly match the "Hit Parade" tunes of Bing Crosby and Wayne King. And when boys talked about the Four Horsemen of the Apocalypse, they weren't discussing the Bible; they were speaking of the football backfield that smashed through all opponents for the glory of Notre Dame.

17

America's youth had plenty of things to occupy their minds, but little or nothing made them curious about religion. For a handful of students at Dallas Theological Seminary, this posed a challenge.

Some of the seminarians were already working a few hours a week for nearby churches. During late night bull sessions, they agreed on one important principle: "We can't wait for teenagers to come to us. We've got to go to them wherever they are— soda fountains, basketball games, street corners, everywhere. We've got to learn to talk with them, to think about things they think about."

Repeatedly Jim used an example from engineering school as they pondered what to do. He'd say, "If you build a bridge and the first time the cars go across, it collapses, you'll never build a bridge that way again." He never understood why Christians didn't see that simple logic. It seemed obvious to him that the bridge had collapsed between the young generation and the church. Every year fewer and fewer made it into the pews. The imperative of Jim's life was to deliver the most beautiful message in the world to as many young people as possible. Anyone who had not responded to the gospel, he figured, must never really have heard it. It would be impossible to catch its incredible beauty and turn it down. More important than anything else was his desire to tell the rebel youngsters outside the church, "God loves you." The greatest tragedy he could imagine was somebody who didn't know he was loved.

Along with his seminary buddies Addison Sewell and Walden Howard, he sought ways to build a bridge to teenagers in the area around Dallas. Across from Fair Park some businessmen helped them put up a tent with a "God Bless America" banner. It was a start. The Christian faith is what made America strong, they reasoned. A kid can't be a good American if he doesn't understand that faith.

Jim did things on the platform in

such a funny way. He was a great joke-teller, a master at getting people's attention, hamming up a Bible story to make it live. "Do you stop having fun when you start talking about Jesus?" he would say. "If you do, God help you."

Simple truth flowed from his words. Excitement leaped through the audience.

4

THE YOUNG couple in the seminary apartment down the hall were intrigued by the Rayburns. Ted and Mary Lou Benson had come from Chicago where Ted worked with the Christian Workers' Foundation. Set up by Herbert J. Taylor, president of Club Aluminum, the Foundation had already invested heavily in InterVarsity Christian Fellowship and Child Evangelism. Now Mr. Taylor was on the lookout for someone to head up an organization for high school students. Benson wrote back, "This fellow Jim Rayburn here has some different ideas on how to reach high school kids. You might want to talk to him."

Mr. Taylor paid Jim's way to Chicago, and talk they did—all day—about novel ways of appealing to teenagers across denominational barriers, and outside the walls of the institutional church. "These ideas sound all right to me, but I don't know if they are the Lord's ideas or yours, Jim. What do you say we try them out?"

Taylor agreed to pay the expenses for a summer tent campaign in Gainesville, sixty miles north of Dallas. Jim's whole theory was to *attract* young people to *Christ* rather than shove them into the church. "Half of our so-called testifying is done to closed hearts and minds," he would say. "People have shut up like clams because somebody made a dumb approach."

He'd learned that lesson the hard way in Chama, New Mexico, where there hadn't been a pastor for twenty-eight years. Jim had found the town shut up, the people's ears plugged. Eventually he discovered why. A young man fresh out of school came to town, hoping to be pastor of the church there. On a busy Saturday morning he would pick out some individual on Main Street and shout to him across the street, "Mr. Barr, are you saved?" It had taken Jim six months of very patient effort in Chama to persuade even one man to let his children go to Sunday school. Five words hurled insensitively had shut the ears and hearts of the whole town against the gospel. "It takes more time now in most places to break down the barriers," Jim had said to Mr. Taylor. "They have to be broken down by love alone. I wonder why it's such a strange idea that we should be nice to lost folks. The Lord Jesus was."

Add and Wally worked with Jim that summer, along with several other seminarians, and the Gainesville experiment proved their methods sound. Each month Jim sent a bill to Herb Taylor in Chicago, along with a report of what was happening. He believed that if God wanted something done it could be done. "It takes that for a pioneer," Mr. Taylor smiled at Jim, "and you'll make a good one." At the same time he kept something else to himself. "I didn't think he'd make such a good leader in developing others," he confessed years later. "As an older man I felt he might be lacking as an administrator."

The pastor of the Gainesville Presbyterian Church was also watching young Rayburn. When he asked Jim to come work with him as a youth minister, Clyde Kennedy explained, "I don't want you to come here just to feed our church kids. I expect you to do whatever is necessary to get to the ones I never see in church. You don't have to make it part of our Presbyterian program." That sounded all right to Jim; Kennedy seemed to understand.

The fall of 1939, Jim's senior year at seminary, he began driving to Gainesville every weekend. Saturdays were good for seeing football games and hanging around wherever the kids were. Sometimes he would meet parents. Always there was time for prayer. Nights he would be invited to stay with one of the families. Sundays he was at the church teaching a class, occasionally preaching when Clyde was gone. Monday was club day.

Jim would amble over to the high school about the time

classes were over and get a few kids to meet with him in one of the classrooms. "What a drag!" Loveta Murphy later leveled with him. "I couldn't think of anything worse than going to something *at* school, after school was over!" Her friends kept trying to sell her on the Young Life club, but it wasn't until the next year that she finally gave in and went with them—just to get them off her back. "That was my first introduction to Jim. He was teaching a chapter from the Gospels. I was fascinated by what I heard. Excited. I didn't have to be asked back."

While that was Loveta's first response to Jim, Add Sewell couldn't see anyone but Vetie. "Wow! What a chick!" he thought. "She sure is painted up." That was in the days when it was very unspiritual to wear lipstick, and Vetie wore a lot.

Without knowing it, Loveta Murphy was acting out two of the basic discoveries which would finally dawn on Young Life about kids anywhere: one, don't try to get them to stay after school for a meeting, if you want them to do what they like to do. And, two, kids will go where their friends are. Vetie not only gave in eventually to her friends' invitation to come to club, but several months later she walked into club bringing the whole football team with her! That was the third thing they had tumbled to—if you can interest the leaders in the school, other kids will follow. Four, evening was a better time to meet; and five was simply that kids were more comfortable in the informal atmosphere of a home than they were in either school or church.

"It was a real concession in those days," Loveta recalled, "for parents to let kids out on a school night. But we liked it a lot better, and the clubs began to boom."

There was backtalk, and there were interruptions, and some of the boys had to fire pillows back and forth across the room, while others looked bored. Singing they did fairly well. It released energy, and it was fun even when they didn't know the songs. One night the star pitcher of the baseball team appeared in the doorway only because his girl had dragged him there. To his surprise he found Jim's talk opening up thoughts that had been secret, thoughts about God and life and himself that he had never expressed. After the meeting, he asked Jim what he meant by "giving yourself to Christ."

"Which would you rather do?" Jim asked. "Play baseball or watch it from the stands?"

5

WHILE THE seminarians had experimented with tying into the structure of an existing Texas youth organization called Miracle Book Club, they gradually saw that God was expecting them to cut their own milestones.

Every Monday night Jim drove back to Dallas from Gainesville. He'd head directly to the men's dorm and go down the hall rapping on doors. Add. Wally. George. Tim. Glen. Ed. Grant. All the fellows would pile onto the bed or sit on the floor in one of the cramped, cell-like rooms, and Jim would tell them what had gone on in club—how the message had been received, which kids had trusted the Lord. Then they would pray.

"It was always exciting," Add said. "We'd never seen anything like it. We had some good clubs going in Dallas and Houston, but none were quite like Jim's. We believed in intensive, extended intercessory prayer in those days. And things were popping!"

By April the club spun off new clubs in several other towns—Gainesville High was cramming 125 kids into the living room where they met—and Jim recorded, "What a club! What a victory the Lord has wrought. Most amazing to see all the worldly and otherwise indifferent-to-the-gospel youngsters that come."

All that year Jim had been talking about the life Christ offers, and Jim embodied the life he talked about. "What still sticks with me," Loveta thought back, "is that God is in the business of giving people life. There was an excitement about the kind of life Jim lived. And I wanted it at any cost."

The kind of life he offered was not typical, but it was particularly appropriate that year in the Gainesville club. Before

22

Add and Loveta

the year was over, Loveta was to experience a traumatic car accident. Several kids were hospitalized. One died. Vetie's pretty face was a network of stitches. Jim and Add made trips up to the hospital to see her several times. Once the seminary quartet went along to sing. Several of the fellows wrote notes and sent cards.

"They were such an encouragement," Vetie shook her head at the memory. "I'd never had anyone take such a personal interest in me. It made a big difference . . . having my face messed up was hard to take. I was very self-conscious, and it made me internalize what was important about my life. I thought a lot about what I did to make myself happy—having friends, being popular and active in all kinds of school activities, getting good grades. Instead of being occupied with just the external, I began to see that it was what went on inside me that was important. It was exciting just knowing that I was forgiven and had life. Two kinds of life! It lit a fire under me."

Inch by inch the seminarians were feeling their way. By the end of that year several other things had been proven. It was very plain that young people did not bypass the church because they disliked hearing about Jesus—what seemed to bother them was the boxed-up feeling of the whole ecclesiastical system. What they responded to was personal friendship, people who cared about what was happening to their lives. And there was no question about the fact that they surely did like it when adults talked to them about something positive, something worthwhile that could lead them beneath the surface of their daily routine into the secret thoughts they had never put into words. In later years Jim told the staff, "I hit the kids where

23

they live. If there's anything American kids are interested in, it's life . . . and they don't much care what they have to do to get it. It's important. It's fascinating. It's compelling. So we talk about life. We don't talk about sin until later. You'd be surprised how easy it is to talk about sin after you talk awhile about real life—who Jesus is and what He has done. My! how they respond to the sinner part then!"

This was a touch of newness that came from heaven. They didn't think it up themselves. They were just open to catch it when it arrived.

6

No LONGER associated with Miracle Book Club, the leaders were considering what to call themselves during the summer tent campaigns coming up. "Good News" sounded all right. "Best Seller" wasn't bad. "Young Life Campaign" appealed to them more than any other, but it was already being used by a youth organization in England led by a Reverend and Mrs. Wood who had visited the campus that year. Upon inquiry, they received word from the Woods that they saw no problem in sharing their name with the Dallas group, and the signs went up on the tent, "Young Life Campaign—Hear Jim Rayburn." Years later Jim laughed, "It didn't mean a thing to the people on the street. But we rather liked the aggressive feel of the word *campaign*."

From Gainesville to Houston to Dallas the summer campaigns crescendoed. Choir rehearsals and crowds, radio broadcasts and roof-garden rallies, catching trains and meeting schedules kept them running through the days, and praying into the early morning hours.

Herb Taylor was still giving generously to whatever Jim got going. "I'm passing on to you cold figures," Jim reported in a

letter of appreciation that summer, "because I think they tell the story. Some Christian workers disagree on this point, but I count very strongly on numbers. A stationary work is a stagnant work. If our work is attractive, it will attract. If it doesn't, we have to know so we can ditch it and start something else that will." When they discovered that some religious clichés were turning kids away from the Savior, they had to find new words that would make him clearly visible.

When the campaigns rolled to a halt at the end of August, everyone was due for a rest. Jim piled four of the men into his new 1940 Pontiac and took off to the Arizona mountains. He was proud of his red automobile just nine days out of the showroom. He was proud too of the rugged West where he and Maxine had learned to trust God. He was eager, above all else, to show off the wonders of the desert—its exhaustion and its satisfaction—to these men who shared his vision.

They drove all night, reaching the valley overlooking Albuquerque at sunrise. The car performed beautifully and Jim relaxed in the back seat while the others drove. Just north of Flagstaff that evening Jim took the wheel. This was his country. He left the road, driving through the lava beds to show it off. Heady with the excitement of being at home again, he raced through the cinders, ignoring his companions' fears of what might happen. "Stick with me, fellas!" he laughed cockily. "I know where I'm going." He started down a slope, heedless of the guys' yells, "Don't go down there, Jim!" He turned halfway in his seat and laughed again, "Aw, I know what I'm doin'."

But Jim didn't know, not at all. The bumpers suspended the car in the loose lava so the wheels couldn't grab, and with no traction, they came to a complete standstill. It took until 10:30 that night to find someone with a tow truck who was crazy enough to drive part way down the slope to rescue the car. With a hundred-yard chain, he was finally able to free the Pontiac from its lava prison.

"We seldom saw Jim cowed by anything," Add commented, "but this night he was quiet, and the next morning he was sick with a migraine headache. I guess those of us who were in on the whole thing sort of took a perverse enjoyment in it. It was one of the few times that anybody got the best of Jim."

7

SHORTLY AFTER they returned from the West, Jim was asked by Dr. Chafer to speak to the Seminary Chapel about Young Life Campaign. It was a momentous day. Sixty-five fellows got fired up enough to come to a meeting the next day to hear more. "We wanted to find out what was so different," Ed Wichern said. "Jim always had the ability to win people over. His enthusiasm was contagious." About forty of them stuck with him all winter in a regular Wednesday afternoon class on Young Life methods. Out of that session a number of club leaders developed. They were followers. Jim was the leader. It was the mood of the day to follow. Within two weeks after the class began, Jim had the fellows out with him making contacts with the kids in the small towns around Gainesville and south in the Houston

Left, George Cowan. Right, Orville Mitchell (in white), Ed Wichern.

area. Most of the men didn't know what they were getting into, but they were moved by Jim's confidence.

On Mondays they drove to Gainesville, dropping off one at a time at Lake Dallas, Valley View, Myra, and Saint Jo. Then as the club was over at the farthest point, they reversed the process and collected all the club leaders on their way back to Dallas. After class on Thursdays, five of them piled into Jim's car and left at one o'clock for Houston, 240 miles away. They were invited to dinner by some of the interested parents who had shared in the summer tent campaign. Then they scattered to various parts of the city to meet with the kids who showed up for club. Reconvening, they drove the 240 miles back to Dallas, catching whatever naps they could before class the next morning.

"My most vivid memory," said George Cowan, "is of the prayer times we had as we rode along—at times hours on end. We would lose all track of time. Often we would unburden our hearts and express our concerns for individual kids. The overall experience was always one of pleasure, even though we often would be beat and baffled over clubs that weren't going right. Jim would never come down on us. All of us were suffering along together trying to find out how to do our job."

December 24, 1940, was a red-letter day in the development of the Campaign. "Today we organized our official Young Life board of directors," Jim recorded in his journal. "Mr. John E. Mitchell, chairman; Ted Benson, secretary-treasurer; Dr. Chafer. Wonderful spirit. Mr. Mitchell gave $200. It's a marvelous blessing—the money, yes, but this man's confidence in the work is the greatest gift."

27

8

THE MITCHELL brothers, John and Orville, had first come to Jim's attention when they stopped by the "God Bless America" tent across from Fair Park. They liked what they saw; Rayburn seemed to know what he was doing. They stayed to nail some benches together for the Campaign, figuring maybe their own kids might even show up to sit on them. Orville and his wife were there almost every night with both their sons. Young Bob Mitchell thought the choir singing "If you take my Jesus" was the "prettiest music" he'd ever heard. And after listening to Jim's low-pressure explanation of how Jesus helped so many people, Bob responded to Jim's invitation and asked Christ into his heart. Forty years later Bob was to become executive director of this same organization that had grown to a $15 million operation.

"Jim made the Scripture take on its true meaning for Frances and me too," Orv wrote in tribute. "As we listened to the gracious words, she said to me, 'We've been called out of darkness into His marvelous light!' "

Leaders in the cotton machinery manufacturing business, the Mitchells were well respected in Dallas business circles. There were countless times after that campaign when God would call on their influence and ability to get his work done.

Almost immediately the scout cabin at the rear of Orville's home was turned into a center where Jim could hang out with the "roughnecks" who especially challenged his ingenuity. Then "Old Club 37" (the first club in Dallas, since who would ever come to "Club Number One"?) took off in the same cabin. Without too much danger of contradiction, Orville Mitchell would go down in history as the first adult volunteer to take over the upfront leadership of a Young Life club. His life became open and vulnerable (and, incidentally, rich) as he earned the right to share himself and his faith with hundreds of Dallas high school students over two generations.

It was the Mitchells who helped Maxine set up the first office of the Campaign in the basement of the men's dorm at the seminary. And it was the Mitchells four years later who pulled it out of the basement and detached it from the seminary altogether. It was the second floor of their newly renovated commercial building in downtown Dallas that they rented to Young Life. "In this office," Orv remembered, "we prayed for our first Young Life camp property. Brother John and I felt there were only two men on the board who believed the Lord would provide an answer to our prayers: Jim Rayburn, a man of faith and vision; and Herb Taylor, a man who had the faith *and* the money."

9

WE USED TO sit over at the Rayburns' house trying to decide the best strategy to reach the world," Wally explained. He was shuffling through hundreds of snapshots of the first leaders and their club kids in every pose imaginable. "We figured in ten years we were really going to change the church . . . and then we would change the world."

Jim couldn't conceive of any greater transmitting station than Dallas Seminary from which to send out men who understood the gospel as Dr. Chafer had crystallized it. He saw Dallas as the "Jerusalem" of Young Life. Mr. Taylor had expanded Jim's vision by telling him, "You'll have to go national, Rayburn, or I'll not give you another dime."

"I remember the night we put newsprint on the floor and got down on our hands and knees, drawing out north, south, east and west, with Dallas at the hub." Add was to go east to Tyler because two Presbyterian pastors there were interested. Wally would go west to Wichita Falls. George and Gordon would move south to Houston. North would have to wait.

By the end of August, they pulled together their first camp. Jim was in his element. He worked the kids out from breakfast until bedtime, having them memorize Scripture. "We'd all stand up," said Roy Riviere, one of Add's fellows from Tyler, "and start saying the second chapter of Second Timothy together. You had to sit down when you couldn't repeat any more."

There were two morning meetings, an enforced rest period when the campers actually had to get back on their beds, and afternoon recreation. Then after supper they had an evening meeting, and then an after-meeting! The only reason they succeeded at all was that they believed God could love kids through them. Often after the campers were bedded down, the counsellors gathered in an empty cabin or around a campfire and prayed that God would come through their efforts and that He would show them better ways to let kids know they were loved.

One night one of the men needed to talk about his own uncertainty. He had been invited to join a growing company of linguists who were translating the Bible into unwritten tribal languages. He felt a growing conflict. George Cowan, who twenty-five years later became president of Wycliffe Bible Translators, remembers how readily Jim caught the significance of the Wycliffe methods—having to learn the language of the native people in order to win a hearing, adapting to their lifestyle in order to live naturally among them and make it easy for them to be at ease. Jim saw what they were having to do with the high school crowd as a parallel situation—the whole idea of "to the Jew, becoming as a Jew, and to the Greek, as a Greek." Under the full moon, kneeling on the grassless earth, George was drawn toward Wycliffe, and was given the blessing of his Young Life associates around the campfire embers.

During his early days as a translator in Mexico, Cowan's only promised support came from his campaigners in the Dallas high schools. Losing one of their own to another mission was one of the ways they struggled to translate Christ's commission in the Book of Acts into their own plans. "You shall be witnesses in Jerusalem, in Judea and Samaria, and to the ends of the earth."

10

IN THOSE pre-war days, they experienced failure as well as success. "Jim kept cheering us up," one associate said, "telling us that by trial and error we were learning. You have to fail sometimes so that you know which mistakes to avoid in the future."

They were not entirely to blame if they could not always focus young people's attention on God. Teenage girls in their long skirts and bobby sox were dancing to "Mairzy Doats and Dozy Doats and Liddle Lamzy Divey" while their boyfriends dropped their allowances a nickel at a time into jukeboxes.

With four full-time staffers busy in clubs, Jim's role changed to that of a fund-raiser. He and Ted Benson traveled as far east as Philadelphia in an effort to keep the young organization alive. Jim was still as convincing as he had been in Chicago with Herb Taylor; only now he could point to what God was actually doing in the lives of boys and girls as he explained the ministry of the Campaign to potential donors. Within a short time, they returned with enough cash and pledges for the Directors to approve a monthly budget of $893! This would make it possible for each of the full-timers to receive a salary of $100 a month.

The next thing the board of directors did was incorporate so that the Campaign could be a tax-exempt organization to which people could contribute as they did to their own churches. Moreover, Texas law required the incorporators to be citizens of Texas. Once again they looked to the Mitchell brothers, whose Texas lawyers drew up the proper documents and filed them October 16, 1941. Young Life was now a bona fide incorporated organization.

Then came the Japanese attack on Pearl Harbor. With thousands of boys going off to fight, and maybe die, thousands of parents hurried off to church—some for the first time in years—to pray for the safety of their sons. At Los Alamos American scientists raced against their German counterparts to see which nation could first produce an atom bomb capable of annihilating hundreds of thousands of human beings in a single blast.

The young of America reacted in ways of their own. Boys, facing military induction at age eighteen, watched older brothers march off and knew they would soon follow. Girls, often left alone as their mothers joined defense workers at Lockheed or Boeing, returned home after school to a house key under the doormat. Others hung around the USOs or waited to enlist in the WACs or WAVES. They wore sloppy Joe sweaters and run-down loafers . . . knitted scarves and socks for soldiers they would never see . . . and swooned as they listened to Frank Sinatra.

Yet God was not entirely forgotten by America's young. Many went to church with their parents; and everywhere the prayer rose: Grant us peace, O eternal source of peace.

A few Texas citizens found that this growing youth organization was posing a threat to their established religious procedures. It appeared to be divisive and arrogant. It was conducted outside the churches. It seemed a deliberate flaunt in the face of the clergy. By what right could these young club leaders assume they were better fitted to speak out for Christ than the ordained ministry? What possible motivation could they have for giving up the admiration of an established congregation and the prestige of the pulpit?

"I'm sure we were obnoxious," Roy Riviere confessed. "We felt so strongly that if you wanted to do something for God, this was it. I'm sure we must have offended a lot of people

32

Jim chauffeurs Jeep-load of kids to top of Pike's Peak.

because we felt we were the most privileged people on earth. Anybody who wasn't on board with us was doing a secondary thing, a less important ministry. We really thought there was nothing else on earth that was as glorious a task as ours. Jim would say, 'This is a marvelous bandwagon we've got on that has just started, and it's going to gather steam. We're going places, and we're going to do great things for God—things nobody's ever done before.' Part of it was youth, just the brashness of youth."

As a high school senior, Roy was brash enough to bike through the pre-dawn streets of Tyler to the funny little apartment where the Sewells lived on the far side of town. To pray with Add for an hour before school gave Roy a sense of involvement in the Kingdom of God that was overwhelmingly new. It was worth almost any energy he could put out for it. After college Roy got on "the marvelous bandwagon" himself.

A number of others who might have come aboard went instead into the armed forces, forcing Young Life to seek for leadership in other places. This served to diversify the profile of the staff, bringing fresh enthusiasm and new perspectives from a variety of religious backgrounds.

One of the new men was a burly football player who came from Baltimore to enter the seminary. George Sheffer had no thought of joining Young Life. He was headed for the ministry, preferably in a Presbyterian church back home. It was his bass voice that changed his direction. Jim asked him to be a part of a volunteer quartet, and in the Rayburn manner he devised a way George could become an entertainer as well. "Let's have some fun," Jim said one day when the fellows were rehearsing. "George, see if you can't sort of growl the bass part. The worse you sound the better the kids will like it."

George did and the kids broke up. "Jim would introduce me as an opera star," George laughed. "I'd take a deep breath and then let out with a croak." It was great fun wherever they repeated the act. "But the most important thing as far as I was concerned," he remembered, "was what was happening to *me*. Going to clubs and rallies, talking with kids, I was coming to understand what Young Life was trying to do—and man! I was hooked."

What George Sheffer did not anticipate was the abruptness with which he was thrust into the operations of the group or what God was going to put him through in the years ahead. When he told Jim he wanted to help out, Jim immediately said, "How about going up to Tonkawa, Oklahoma, to start a club?" At Tonkawa, George found a willing pastor to introduce him to the high school principal. Before the end of the week, he had found some cooperative parents who agreed to open their homes for a club meeting. The Mackenzies had a teenage boy who was dreaming of becoming a Big Ten football star. "When he found out that I had played football, he became my closest buddy," said George. "His family even asked me if I'd like to move in

George Sheffer, bottom left.

with them. I did, and by the end of summer their home was such a beehive of kids we had to look for a bigger meeting place."

With this club thriving, George was off to start another in Oklahoma City. Arriving in the afternoon, he got off the bus and started walking. He'd never been there before. He knew nobody in the city. After a few blocks he stopped to ask himself: Where am I going? What do I do now?

On a far corner he saw a drugstore. There he looked in the classified telephone directory and began phoning churches. Most of them took no interest in his project. "We have our own youth program," he was told.

He made a dozen calls, his spirit sinking lower with each one. Then the pastor of a small Baptist church said, "Young Life? Oh, yes, I know about them. Why don't you come over here so we can talk. I think quite a few folks around here would like the idea."

11

ONCE A CLUB got going in one place, it acted as a wedge to open other communities. Jim would hang around a high school until someone finally asked him, "What do you do, Jim?" And he'd say, "I lead Young Life clubs."

"Young Life clubs?"

"Yeah. Haven't you ever heard of Young Life?"

"No."

"And you think you're somebody, don't you?"

Of course they'd never heard of it—there weren't any clubs in their town. So he'd lead them on. "It's the greatest thing going! In Tyler High School a hundred kids come to club every week. You don't know about it?" Then he'd set up a time with them. "Tell you what. Get your girls and meet me Tuesday night. We'll have supper together at the hotel, and I'll tell you about it."

Usually they showed up. The appeal was a winner with kids—a constant kind of daring to find out what he was talking about.

Another thing Jim tried was high school assemblies. Wherever the staff men made a contact they would also line up an assembly date for Jim with the principal. Sheffer described the way Jim worked: "He really wowed the kids. He had such a shy, quiet approach. He was marvelous building up to the punchline. Like, 'High school isn't so bad, is it? It's just the principal of the thing.' Kids would cheer and whoop and howl. Then he'd go on about 'that cross-eyed teacher they had to fire because she couldn't see eye to eye with her pupils.' He was corny as could be the first half. Then he'd talk about the fact that our nation was based on the Christian faith, and there was a heritage in our country that a lot of kids didn't know anything about. 'You're doing yourselves a disservice,' he'd say, 'if you don't at least find out what you're missing.' "

It was a dare, a challenge. Don't be ignorant. Don't turn thumbs down on the greatest proposition in the world until you've checked it out.

It was an era when authority was not doubted. Children didn't question parents when they were told to do something. Leadership was not questioned. Jim's approach left high school students with a feeling of awe.

Part of the technique was to find quality people who could be paraded as hero models before the high school assemblies. Gil Dodds was one. At that time he held the world's indoor record in running the mile. And he was a Christian. He traveled with Jim through Texas, Colorado, and on to the west coast. Jim would warm up the crowd with his humor, then a couple of fellows would step out just as Gil was introduced and unfurl a huge banner with dozens of his medals pinned on it. Then Gil would humbly tell his story. Dodds was the first miler to run against the clock. Rather than competing against other runners, he was always stretching to pull out the best that God had built into him. That afternoon he would run on the high school track with any of the kids who wanted to be with him. Sometimes the kids would come back for an evening meeting, and they would hang on every word Gil said.

Gil Dodds, left

In some cities they would cram in five or six assemblies in a day. After one of those days Jim was heard saying, "One of the reasons I'm eager to get to heaven is to see if these things do any good."

Gradually they began to feel uneasy about these big rallies. What about all the kids who were coming to Christ? Quite a few did in each place. "But we were always moving on. We weren't spending time with them," Sheffer said, "and we began to see that this might not be the best route to go."

Without knowing it, they were stumbling onto another significant—and very scriptural principle—one that would sweep America in twenty-five years. It was simply this: their own lives had been influenced firsthand by the lives of other people who cared—the sort of thing Loveta felt when Jim drove sixty miles to visit her in the hospital—and they were needing to be equally in touch with those kids who had accepted Christ in the assemblies. It was the inclusive experience of one person's being vitally present to another in an ongoing commitment—as Roy felt when he prayed with Add in the early morning before school. This seemed to be the thing that made more lasting difference than the dynamic preaching to hundreds or thousands.

37

"Where our little canoe was going," Roy mused, "had very little relation to how we were paddling. In the middle of many things we didn't have the faintest notion if they would work. It was a trial-and-error matter that was bathed in prayer and that contained a fierce determination for excellence. When something did work it often surprised us. Later we'd go back and ask why. A lot of times we could find good answers because the grace of God utilizes laws and reason and principles."

12

THE TOPSY-TURVY dispersal out of Dallas into such faraway places as Bellingham, Washington, and Memphis, Tennessee, brought an end to much of the day-to-day fellowship which had knit the staff so closely together. Camps and staff conferences became means of reestablishing some of that contact.

The first camp at Tejas (near Denton, Texas) was crude and drab, but it gave staff leaders a chance to be in continuous communication with their club kids for a concentrated week. At that time the Board was willing to rent the facilities for the whole summer.

Camp Tejas was a far cry from Jim's burning desire for a site that would match his gusto for life. He constantly sought ways to share what he loved to do. God had blended his job with exactly the kind of life he would have chosen, if he had no job. His enthusiasm signaled a very clear message, "Here is the neatest thing I know to do in all the world, and I'm going to take you along with me to do it."

Much of Jim's love of adventure sprang from his early family vacations in the Rockies. He had hiked those mountains from childhood, and the yearning to return kept him looking for a future beyond the Texas lowlands.

By mid-1945, plans were laid to take all forty staff people to

Manitou Springs, Colorado, for a two-week conference in the old Navajo Hotel. It was the first chance Jim had to share his vision of a campsite in the Rockies with any of them. He hiked them first from the top of Mt. Manitou over past Crystal Park, because this was one of his favorite places. Then he took them overnight to the top of Pike's Peak. It was a strenuous climb, but they all made it. Some were excited, others just plain sick. However, Jim had succeeded in giving them an unforgettable experience of the awesome majesty he felt in the mountains, and he expected they would start praying with him about a piece of property that Young Life could some day own.

Jim waited no longer than the day after the staff left Manitou to see an attorney about buying Crystal Park. "He had no idea how we could get such a place," Maxine said. "He was almost scared to talk seriously about Colorado because he loved it so much. We were aware that we might be putting our wishes above God's."

*First staff conference
in Colorado*

*Gloria and
Herb Taylor*

For several weeks afterwards, everything worked in Jim's favor. The owners were not only open to selling, they even suggested cutting the $30,000 price. Mr. and Mrs. Taylor flew out from Chicago to look over the site and made a bid on the spot. Then a few days later Jim got a phone call from the realtor in Colorado Springs. The message? Crystal Park had been sold to someone else.

The vision of the Rockies faded as they got caught in the crunch of the mission's financial crisis. Even though they were going weeks without salaries, they were amazed to discover God's provision in the lack. The girls in the Dallas office found there was never a day they couldn't come up with at least fifty cents among them. Sometimes one of them would receive a letter with a dollar bill inside. That would feed all four girls that day on a head of lettuce and a can of soup, with some left over. One of the girls recalls living on cornflakes once for five days—without milk. Another tried apples and peanuts. The most remarkable thing about those payless days was not the lack of food, but the closeness that lack brought to the girls. Kay MacDonald, who had left a good job in Memphis to come to Young Life, said, "It pulled us together and it pulled us to the Lord. We knew what our common source was. It was a very concrete experience of God's blessing—not just in the intangibles of a club meeting. It was what do I eat today, Lord?"

There was not enough money to meet the budget that September as the fiscal year ended. The policy at the time was simply to wipe out the deficit if salaries were not paid up, and start with a clean slate October 1. "We needed $2500, as I recall," Kay continued. "We all went to the cabin at the back of Mitchells' house and spent the day praying. We'd read something, then get down on our knees and pray, then read some more and pray some more." At one point the phone rang.

It was H. J. Taylor in Chicago. "I couldn't get away from the feeling that I should call and let you know I'm sending $2500 to you today."

13

LOSING CRYSTAL PARK had been a blow, but Rayburn, being the man he was, could only translate it into expectations of something better. At the board meeting the next spring, camp property was discussed and considerable interest aroused in the Rocky Mountain area. President Taylor was fired by the vision of seven million high school kids in America, and the knowledge that only ten thousand of them were being reached by Young Life. "We must increase our workers," he declared. "Picture a hundred staff workers, with a dozen unpaid volunteers apiece, doing the actual contact work with the kids." A thousand clubs was the goal they set.

Shortly after that meeting, Mr. Taylor had a call from Jim. "I know now why the Lord didn't want us to have Crystal Park. We've found something better. It's all complete, ready to move into. It's a beautiful spot. I want you and Mrs. Taylor to fly out here and take a look at Star Ranch."

When the Taylors landed in Colorado Springs, Jim was nowhere around. They waited and then decided to drive south of the city and look at the ranch without him. It was on the market

Star Ranch

for $100,000; but by the time Mr. Taylor got through dickering over the valuable spur collection, the fancy chandeliers, and the furniture—all of which were too elegant for kids—the price was cut in half. Eager to make a deal, Taylor drew up an agreement with the lady who was handling the property. "I don't have this much with me," he said, "and I'm not buying it for myself— we'll have to have a board meeting. But I'd like to give you a check for $1000, and we'll put this up with a bank in the Springs. If I don't pay the other $49,000, it's your $1000." She agreed and Taylor wrote her a check. After dropping it at the bank, the Taylors went back to the Broadmoor Hotel for dinner. Jim was there, full of apologies, thinking he had blown the whole deal because his plane had been grounded in Texas. When he stopped explaining long enough to listen, Mr. Taylor told him, "We just bought Star Ranch."

Back in Chicago, Taylor called a special board meeting because the balance of the money was due in thirty days. "The board wasn't interested at all," Taylor recalled. "In the first place they didn't have that much money, and they didn't know where we could get it. Another thing they said was that Jim just likes mountain climbing, and he likes skiing and that's why he wants that ranch. They even told me, 'Taylor, kids won't go to the mountains. Kids from Texas wouldn't want to do that. Kids from New York or Bellingham will never go there.' There wasn't a one who would vote for it. I was stuck with my $1000 gone, and no $49,000 to take over the balance. And the worst thing was that I knew it was a wonderful buy!"

The Mitchell brothers were astounded that Taylor would share Jim's faith about this camp expense at a time when they were struggling over money to pay staff salaries. Taylor left the board meeting, sold his preferred stock in Club Aluminum, and bought Star Ranch himself.

Five miles southwest of Colorado Springs the ranch nestled up against Cheyenne Mountain. Jim believed it was the most beautiful property he had ever seen for a young people's camp. In his report to the board he wrote, "Mr. Taylor will incorporate the Christian Camp Foundation of Colorado to lease this beautiful campus and all the buildings and surrounding territory to the Young Life Campaign for $1 a year, for the purpose of conducting a full-scale summer program for young people, and for our leadership and staff training. Everyone who sees it is unanimous in believing it is the Lord alone who has saved this ranch for us, and in His own good time has given it to us."

A month later they took possession, and an impromptu crew converged on Star Ranch to celebrate—and to prepare for the staff conference coming up in two weeks. They were hilarious in their excitement. They bought bunk beds from Fort Carson and spray-painted them . . . repaired and repainted old furniture which they collected around the ranch and made usable . . . cleared ground for a baseball diamond and a volleyball court. The Taylors sent aluminum utensils for the kitchen. They improvised tables with boards on sawhorses, and Wanda Ann Mercer was about to go into the Springs to buy oilcloth to cover the boards.

43

Top: Star Ranch; Dick Langford, left, Wally Howard, in swing. Bottom left: Wally and Wanda Ann Mercer. Bottom right: Bob Mitchell.

"No, you are not!" Jim called out. "Buy tablecloths."

"But Jim, tablecloths have to be laundered, and we don't have a laundry."

"Well, we're not going to eat off of oilcloth at this camp!"

They had tablecloths from the very first meal. They slept on the floor all that week, but they ate in style.

"Best investment I ever made," Herb Taylor chuckled thirty years later, as he did a little figuring. "Probably thirty thousand kids heard the gospel at Star since we bought it. That's about a dollar and a half apiece."

14

THE START OF the Colorado camping program was a key to the rapid expansion of Young Life beyond a provincialism into a national influence. Kids arrived at Star from all over the country. As with everything before, the staff was stumbling into the germ of an idea that put them on the road to discovering God's greater idea.

Camp was operated on a couple of principles that were unlike most other camps of the day. One—instead of having a main speaker to attract kids, Jim insisted that the counselor was the key person in making camp an effective experience. Rather than being leader-centered, it was individualized. The counselors became God's links to the six or eight boys or girls assigned to their cabins. The whole idea was for the counselor to spend time with them. Do things with them. Get to know them. Share personal enthusiasms with them.

The other key was quality. In a day when lean-tos, tent houses, and meager surroundings were synonymous with most

Christian conference grounds, Jim believed in excellence. Anyone who was part of the early work remembers the sound of Jim's concern, "Who started the idea that Christians ought to have camp in tents? We talk about the King of kings; let's act like He's in charge! We're going to have the classiest camps in the country."

This concept opened Young Life to more critical stabs. In strange contrast to its humble beginnings, it came to be mocked in a number of churches as "a rich man's game."

Within three years the facilities at Star Ranch were too small, and another place a hundred miles west and two thousand feet higher was added. This time the cabins were run-down, but the hot water swimming pool could not be surpassed. The springs ran so abundantly that European nobility had bathed there for almost a century.

The first staff assigned to Silver Cliff, then called the Byrd Colony, agreed that it was historic . . . but it was also antique. The way they got kids to come there the first summer was to bring them over bodily by bus from Star Ranch after that camp was filled up. George Sheffer ran the first season. "Everything was wrong. The cabins needed repairs. The sewers didn't work. The place was a dust bowl. But we knew one thing, and I thank God for everybody who was there and caught it. We didn't have the quality layout but we sure had the love of Christ! All of the counselors agreed, 'Let's love these kids.' And I bet there wasn't another group of campers anywhere who had such a total reaction as camp ended, 'I don't wanna leave. This is the greatest place I've ever been.' "

A third factor in the uniqueness of the camping program was the work crew. This was a core of mature Christian kids who were eager to work out their commitment to the Savior by sharing what they had experienced with new kids who had no idea how good life could be. The crew was selected from clubs on the basis of willingness to serve and readiness to grow. Out of a spring class of fifteen to twenty applicants, each local leader would choose one or two to go to the ranches. There they worked without pay in one of the tightest bonds of Christian fellowship they would experience in a lifetime. This spirit, demonstrated in every aspect of camp life from washing dishes to climbing the peaks, rarely failed to capture the curiosity of the campers.

15

WATCHING WHAT God was doing in Young Life made it hard to accept what was going on privately with the Rayburns. The summer of 1937 had marked the onset of suffering in a love that was so good it was almost scary. While still in their twenties, Jim and Maxine had experienced miracles and depression butted one against the other in bewildering confusion. Both of them were targets for pain and illness—and the complicating strain of poverty.

The first summer after their move to Texas, Maxine was at the seminary, pregnant, while Jim was hospitalized for six weeks in Albuquerque in critical condition following a ruptured appendix. "I just knew he was going to die," Maxine recalled. "I felt like my heart was breaking. If I go to Albuquerque the doctor says the baby will miscarry, and Jim might not live either, so I won't have anybody. If I don't go and all goes well here, Jim might not live, so I'll have the baby, but I won't have Jim. If I stay here and things go well both places, I'll have both Jim and the baby." She wanted to go out on the highway and flag down the first thing that would take her west. In the only really big decision she had made on her own since their marriage, she decided to stay in Dallas.

By the time Jim returned, he had lost thirty pounds and complications had developed which required more surgeries before proper healing could take place. In the meantime their baby girl was born, a happy interlude before Maxine was plunged into the blackest of depressions. She was diagnosed as having a nervous breakdown. En route to the hospital that fall day, they

47

turned on the radio and heard, "Look down, look down that lonesome road before you travel on." "If we had known the physical suffering and emotional sacrifice that lay ahead of us," Maxine reminisced, "I don't know if we would have gone on."

The migraine headaches which began when Jim was nine years old never completely released their grip on him. Those who worked closely with him knew well the pattern of crippling pain and recovery. Sometimes, driving to a meeting with him, the fellows would massage his neck. Other times he would be so violently ill they would have to stop the car and let him out. The injections were hard for him to take. The medication made him nauseous. But his pattern was to pause briefly, then as soon as relief came, to go on.

Although Jim had learned to accept the headaches as a part of life, he was never free of the quiet, driving search for relief. His journal-keeping over thirty years seemed almost a primary effort to discern the pattern of headache pain and medication and the triumph of the days free from suffering. Code entries at the top of the pages seemed to analyze the sequence of days when he could make it without resorting to medication. It was almost like a contest between two selves. Travel in many cities put Jim in touch with new doctors who attempted to find the solution to the problem, or at least a better way of coping with the intense discomfort. Each time he went for a day longer than normal without the familiar migraine, he was certain he was being released from the nagging burden.

After their second little girl arrived just before Jim's graduation, it became even harder for Maxine to accompany Jim to a club meeting or a weekend. There was no money for a babysitter even when she had the strength and the desire to go. When Jim returned she would often see him so tired or in pain that she was fearful something worse would happen to them. "Somewhere along the line in my lack of experience and ignorance of the Word, I got a notion that if you're really all out for

48

the Lord, you're going to get knocked on the head. I felt shaky. I realized that some people break down when a lot of things pile up, and I began to wonder if I was the type of person who could adjust if Jim continued in this work. I did want him to do what he wanted to do, because I knew a man can't be happy any other way, and I knew enough about being in God's will to know that had to be the most secure place. But something was lacking in me. I had a fuzzy idea about all that was happening."

At thirty-three, Jim found doors opening to him in many places, and he was stretching to keep up with the exploding demands. It seemed to Maxine and the girls that he was away from home at least half the time, and Jim even wondered sometimes—between meetings of all kinds, travel and correspondence—if fatigue might not win out over joy.

His lavish love for life caused him to be deeply bothered when he was out of gear in any way. When he'd have a bad day he'd lament, "Shouldn't have days like this. Don't see how the Lord can be honored in such a day." An experience of misunderstanding sometimes led to blowups with staff members, and he would write in his journal, "I've been pretty much of a mess in just being tough and impatient, lacking kindness and consideration. Failed quite badly in prayer today. Am filled with unrest."

His journal again reveals that great days, great expenditures of energy were usually followed by a weary nonproductive week when it was difficult to get anything done. This unrest would drive him to prayer. "Did not feel like praying but knew I needed to more than anything," he recorded. "As I study this morning I am convinced that the times of coldness and unrest (such as I have had for several days) are always due to failure in prayer and feeding on the Word. . . . I am *out* if I do not *rely* completely on Him." Days of productive encounters, joyous fellowship, rest and blessing invariably followed his return to a proper ordering of priorities. Sometimes it was a series of meetings which were cold and lifeless that would suddenly burst open with responsiveness. Sometimes it was his relationship to Maxine. Occasionally he would refer to the family, "Home is

Rayburn at home with his son

even different lately. The Lord has charge of us. He chose me and He can have me!"

When Maxine delivered a baby boy in the fall of 1945, they called him James. Jim was a proud father, and it was a moving experience, but the work of the Campaign came first as always. It wasn't that Jim didn't love his family; he enjoyed them intensely and needed them to return to from the outside world. But . . . he was a man who was heart and soul given over to the work he was called to do. One of his associates said, "That was all in the world that mattered. It must have been very difficult for his family—that kind of dedication, that kind of compassion for lost kids, his fire. When he was at his best it appeared that he didn't need anybody. It was just Jim and God against the world."

The hint of difference that was a mere shadow during the Arizona days loomed threateningly between Jim and Maxine. Sometimes it seemed that Young Life would founder on the limitations of their humanity. Maxine's illnesses recurred frequently. A back problem gave her such pain there were days when she could not move out of bed to care for the children. At one point they had to hire a full-time nurse. Jim would remain home for a day or two to help, then depart again to find new volunteer leaders for Young Life, and men and women to support the activities.

Maxine cried out that he was more interested in other people's children, that he was on a suicidal course. His health certainly was no better. The headaches tortured him almost daily, and he suffered cold after cold with complicating sinus infections.

"We were both bewildered," Maxine explained in retrospect, "so confused. I kept thinking why in the name of common sense did the Lord choose to put together two people whose feelings were so different. The only way I could figure it out was that I had some qualities Jim needed, and he certainly had a lot I needed. Jim always felt he was doing God's work. He believed that with all his soul. I knew in my heart I had to help him do it even when I rebelled. I guess I made it terribly hard for him. But then, he made it terribly hard for me, too. I heard him talk to others about the sacredness and importance of a man's calling from God. He believed it was such a sacred trust and so private that no other human being had any right to interfere. He became more and more conscious of having been given a great responsibility, and I think it scared him half to death. He was *afraid* to stop working."

16

THE DECADE of the '40s has been called one of the longest, unloveliest in human history. It was a time when discipline and patriotism wielded a strong influence, yet at the same time the war machines kept shoveling young men underground. In the surplus of death, sounds of life had great appeal, and teenage fellows who took the gift that Young Life offered were better prepared to die—or live.

Reports came back from North Africa, France, Germany, and the islands of the Pacific from servicemen who were living by the orders God had given them through Young Life clubs and camps. Van Nall, who had learned to trust God in a Texas club, wrote back after his platoon surrendered to the Germans: "We were half-starved and half-frozen and I'd gone down from 167 to 135 pounds. Sure I got hungry. But one day as I was thinking about a big steak and all the milk I could drink, the Lord gave me a verse: *Take no thought for your life, what ye shall eat, or what ye shall drink: nor yet for your body, what ye shall put on. Is not life more than meat and the body more than clothes? . . . Seek ye first the kingdom of God and his righteousness, and all these things shall be added unto you.* From then I haven't worried about food. God was able to take care of me. I was hungry, but He brought me to fuller understanding of Himself and His way of life for me."

One of the young officers who came out of the Navy after the war enrolled at Wheaton College in Illinois. With the scars of violence and killing gouged in his mind, Bill Starr returned to his education with a strong conviction: only a living out of the life of Jesus Christ could prevent a third world war from demolishing the earth.

On campus he dropped into a group called the Young Life Fellowship. Having grown up around the railroad yards of Chicago and St. Paul, the name meant nothing to him. The people he met there were likable—Bob Mitchell, Roy Riviere, Tom Raley, and several others had apparently been considerably influenced by this thing called Young Life. Bill watched the dozen or so students take up a collection to buy a plane ticket for a man who would fly in from Texas to talk to them. They were so confident of Jim Rayburn's ability to teach them what they needed to know about the Bible and about kids that Bill decided to stick around and find out more.

Most of the fellows and girls were involved in leading clubs in neighboring high schools. Bill, who had led a Hi-C club in St. Paul, got started with them quite easily. For a while Jim flew in and out of Chicago, sharing what he knew with these volunteers who would soon be the new leadership for the entire organization. The principles that had survived the trial and error of the first decade seemed pretty much commonsense to Bill, but in many efforts with young people he knew they were often overlooked: 1) go where kids congregate, 2) accept them as they are, 3) learn how to walk in wisdom to those outside the faith, 4) see the dignity of each unique person, 5) find a neutral setting for the club meeting, 6) create a climate that is informal, 7) speak naturally in terms familiar to the vocabulary of the kids, 8) communicate your certainties rather than flaunt your doubts, 9) consider it a sin to bore kids, especially with the gospel, 10) build on their instinct for adventure, and 11) capitalize on the elements of good humor and music to establish an openness to the gospel.

Looking back over the twenty-eight years that have intervened, Bill sees that this student leadership group formed the spearhead of a warm-hearted volunteer corps that has attracted thousands of men and women since then. "It was opening up an overflow out of the lives of God's people," he says, "not a professionalized witness, but a loving flavor that attracts others to Christ."

Add Sewell and George Sheffer each took a turn at continuing and developing the Fellowship as a training program for both volunteer and full-time staff. They covered everything from the doctrine of the Holy Spirit to the use of a deodorant. It was a different approach for Wheaton, but a memorable one, and has had an impact to this day on many alumni who were on campus at that time.

Wanda Ann Mercer, who was a lively part of that Fellowship, went on to work as Jim Rayburn's secretary. "We gained a view of the world, of God, of Jesus Christ, of people without Christ that is not that which most people have," she says. "It's ingrained in us to react with compassion to people in need. It's so far down deep in us that it's almost instinctive now. It's ingrained in us to think positively about the Christian life and about the will of God—which for the most part makes us basically very happy people, content, optimistic, with hope and faith and joy and love."

Starr explained, "The Fellowship was the start of a much bigger idea in the mind of the Father. It was the utilization of *adults*. God was moving us to challenge mature individuals along their Christian pilgrimage, to provide them an outlet for service—people who were ready and wanting to do something, who had a fullness in their own lives to share, and were eager to join Young Life on a volunteer basis."

Maybe it was a Volkswagen dealer who heard a Young Life talk and wanted to do something. The breakfast meeting he organized for three hundred businessmen turned into a twice-a-year opportunity for Young Life dads to bring their friends to Christ—and also to a better understanding of their own kids.

Or a widow like Vee Whitworth, who found new meaning in life through teaching the Bible to mothers of club kids. Or a schoolteacher couple, like the Haugens, right on the scene with high school students, but looking for better ways of sharing the Savior's love. Or a dentist who long ago decided he could have two lives: Andy Nyboer handles all his patients between 6:30 and 2:30, then puts on his Young Life hat and literally becomes a kid again as he enters into the high school interests and activities in his community. The Nyboers' club attracts two hundred kids, and they keep an expanding pile of letters from those who go away, but can't forget the effect of those two gracious adults on their lives. Then there's the retired Air Force colonel and his wife who say they are happier than they've ever been as part of the leadership team for their high school.

Andy Nyboer

And the public relations administrator who values the training he gets in the leadership classes— "high caliber input that I've experienced nowhere else, a serious equipping for service."

From Orv Mitchell in Dallas to the six thousand men and women across the United States today, volunteers put the gospel on an everyday, down-to-earth level. The idea is that the trained staff leader trains others—he becomes the instructor, the facilitator. The emphasis is not *control* as much as it is *stimulation,* setting in motion. And in the process a team of leaders grows up—a college student, a mother, a real estate agent, a ski-shop owner, a coach, an artist, a corporate vice-president, an insurance underwriter, and on and on.

When Young Life is working efficiently, the people in a community will start saying, "I can't do the kid thing. What can I do?"

17

WHEN STARR and Mitchell arrived at Silver Cliff for Staff Conference (1950), they didn't realize they would learn their biggest lesson from two work crew kids. It was a Texas high school wrangler and a Seattle tennis champ who wandered up the trail almost straight above Silver Cliff and came out on another camp—and a dream that would challenge the whole staff. Clinging to the side of the mountain, Round Up Lodge was almost entirely camouflaged from the road below, but it was well worth a second look. Cy Burris and Jerry Kirk returned the next day on horseback and decided to ask God to give it to Young Life. "We figured God could use it a lot better than those rich boys from the East," Jerry said. For a month the two of them got up early each morning and rode to a big rock near Round Up. There they would stop and spend time with the Lord, believing that He was going to give them that camp. What Cy and Jerry did not know was that the American Camping Association rated Round Up Lodge the finest camp west of the Mississippi!

Mitch smiles as he tells his side of the story. "When we heard what those kids were doing, we counseled them to pray more appropriately and not ask God for stupid things like that— especially right after he'd given us Silver Cliff. It's a wonder we didn't ruin their prayer life. Instead they strengthened ours."

What none of them realized was that Rayburn had been watching Round Up Lodge ever since Ted Benson had mailed

him an ad from the *New Yorker* for a half-million-dollar boys'
ranch in the Colorado Rockies. When Rayburn confirmed the
fact that the ad referred to the same Round Up Lodge, he also
learned that it was, indeed, for sale. The St. Louis physician
who owned the property brought the price down to $300,000,
and on top of that decided to make a $50,000 donation to
Young Life.

Sheffer remembers the board meeting when Jim brought the
matter up, just as the men were putting on their coats to ad-
journ. "OK, Jim," they agreed. "You're free to go ahead on
one condition—you cannot touch the present sources of money.
You'll have to get it entirely funded by new donors."

"I'll never forget walking out of that room," Sheff laughed.
"Jim put his arm around me and said, 'George, it's ours! All
we gotta do is get $250,000. You pray and I'll go get it!' " And
Sheff said, "OK, Jim, 'cause that's sure not my ball game!"

That night on the train en route to Memphis, Jim wrote to
Maxine: "It was one of the very best board meetings we have
ever had. I told them about Round Up and they were bowled
over! And they in turn bowled me over. To my utter amazement,
Mr. Taylor said that the board should officially authorize me to
contact wealthy donors and large foundations for the money.
There was an enthusiastic unanimous vote authorizing the project. Really, honey, although we haven't got Round Up by a long
shot, it was an amazing vote of confidence, and evidence to me
of the Lord leading."

Since it was Maxine's thirty-ninth birthday, he continued, "I
thought of you many times during the day. I've loved you ever
since the first time I saw you. The years of illness have made it
seem at times like that wasn't so . . . but my life has been made
rich by your love. . . . I have thousands of memories of things
I couldn't have had if you hadn't loved a guy starting out the
hard way, at a job he didn't know how to do. I remember years
when we had less materially than ever, and apparently never
lacked a thing because we were so happy about each other.

"And besides that you've given me the sweetest kids in all the
world. Each one of them means more to me than everything else
in the world combined. So, remember, I love you. And I'll bet

you'll be able to pass for thirty-nine for at least another fifteen years, and ten times easier than Jack Benny!"

In thirty days the money was in hand, and Round Up became Young Life's Frontier Ranch, the third campsite in four years. When Jim took some of the staff up to look at Frontier, he carried a long heavy chain of labeled keys. Roy remembered the tour in detail. "We'd walk up to a building, read the name above the door, find the right key, open the door and troop inside. Then we'd look around and stop for a prayer of thanks. We prayed in every building in that place. We were overwhelmed with what God had given us!"

Staff in the early '50s

18

THE ORIGINAL concept that Rayburn had about a club—that it should be "a Christian club for non-Christian kids"—was now being translated into a camping situation. What would a Christian camp for non-Christians be like?

"I remember," Starr said, "seeing a counselor watch kids smoke at the Ranch, and just absolutely die inside—because this was a 'Christian' camp. That left a real impression on me because we were trying to act out the biblical idea of 'Don't judge people.' I thought, 'How can we change their lifestyle unless some new life inside makes them want to change their lifestyle?' "

It was the same beautiful truth again that had burst over Jim twenty years earlier the night he found Chafer's book. How can any of the fruits of a life be changed until the sap that flows through that life is of God?

"We were very, very legalistic in our camps," Bill recalled. "I can remember Annie Cheairs just hopping mad about girls in shorts and skimpy bathing suits. 'No shorts' was the rule. What happened was that our theology began to deepen with our personal experience of Christ. God began to root out our legalism, which was a painful deal.

"It was the same thing about the meetings. Could we trust God to get to kids if we just let them be themselves—even smoking and stuff? And us just being ourselves?"

It was like a silent invasion, shifting slightly, gently, in the direction of *accepting people as they are* and letting the Holy Spirit do the moving in His own time and manner.

"We began to see that, if we took care of our end of things properly, personally, we could trust the Holy Spirit to do his work," Bill said. "I liked the idea that kids didn't feel they were being sucked into a Christian thing. Surrounded by believers, they didn't have any idea what was happening to them. All they knew was they liked being loved and cared for. As they experienced the personal touch, then we could tell them why."

That was the key that Bill Starr picked up—the importance of the people. He was impressed very deeply as he and Bob Mitchell took more and more responsibility in the camps.

"Program isn't the main thing," Bill continued, "but we began to see that program was the *vehicle* to get the main thing—the magnificence of the Savior—to the kids. It wasn't necessarily 'people-oriented' versus 'program-oriented'; it was more how we could use program to make people primary. That was terrific to me. All the beautiful mountain climbing, all the side-splitting entertainment, all the music and the singing were ways to convey the fact that God loves, that *we* love."

At the same time, Rayburn had gradually increased the Bible sessions. Finally, one of the campers went to Mitch and told him he had been to six meetings that day. But, when Mitch would bring it up, Rayburn would retort, "It's up to us to convince them, to sell them. You're the leaders; get out there and lead those kids."

"After everything was over every night," Mitch said later, "there was the seventh meeting. Back to your cabin for Cabin Time, a sort of group devotions. There were specific things we had to do as counselors. I remember sitting on that bunk many nights, trying to get that thing going with kids who weren't even Christians. 'Get out of the head, guys, come on over here.' 'Hey, Joe! Wake up that kid over there.' It had to be quiet—that was one of the rules. But some other counselor would be in the next room with the window open between us and he'd be trying to get something going with his cabin too."

One kid, a high school newscaster, always had his radio on. Competing with his radio got John Carter so frustrated one night that he went outside and pulled the main switch. That turned off the lights, the radio, everything. But by the time he stumbled back into the dark cabin, the kid had switched the radio to battery, and they all just gave up and went to sleep.

Camp was a tough assignment. Jim kept telling them they

59

were supposed to lead, yet all the time they felt they were being led into new discoveries by the kids. It was a dynamic point of tension. "The kids are wrong," Jim would argue. "They don't know what is right. Are you leaders or aren't you?"

Eventually, some of the men just checked out of the old regime and moved on their own convictions. They cut out the Huddle, the Morning Roundup and the rest hour, and they almost lost their jobs in the process! It was a radical transition as they began to see that they were not there to brainwash the kids or to blast them into heaven in one week.

Bill remembered, "We were torn up. We could hardly stand it because we knew the kids were right. The kids were forcing us to look at what was happening. We knew we had to change or we wouldn't have a camp. It took about four years for us to hear what they were saying. It was mostly the non-Christian kids who faced us down."

It was hard to change anything, because Jim was always on the scene. He and the family lived at Frontier Ranch during the summer, and he would bring people in so they could see what was going on.

"He was a spellbinder," Bill continued. "We thought so highly of him that we had bought the whole camp thing just the way he saw it. But living with the kids day after day and trying to make it work Jim's way made us recognize that we couldn't cope with the conflict any longer. I began to see that a lot of what was happening was not due to the Spirit of God, but through our own capacity to change kids. We were selling them on what we were talking about, not allowing a beautiful discovery of the truth of God to take place.

"One morning at Frontier I started getting all our leaders up for a Bible study. (One of the new guys, Dick Lowey, I used to have to drag out every morning, he was such a sack rat!) We were reading in Matthew, the 25th chapter, and I suddenly saw it: *I was meeting Christ in those pagan kids. They were teaching me.* It has had a profound impact on me to this day.

"It became apparent that the leaders weren't only the teachers. *You're teacher and learner always,*" continued Bill. "Nobody's got it all. We were getting directions from the campers' complaints, and more and more this give-and-take became our salvation. God was teaching us to be open, to listen, to take it and to learn.

"We began growing up," said Bill, "when we finally realized people don't get these things cleared up in a night's sleep. We didn't learn all about camping and then do it. We didn't have a great idea about properties, and then plot out how we could buy the right ones. All that gradually occurred. The same with the clubs, the same with communicating the Christian message, the same with training. *I really sense we were Spirit-led to do what we were doing.* We didn't have a thing to do with it, except to be there. It wasn't any of us sitting down and figuring out, 'How do we get with teenagers?' "

Looking back now, it is easy to see that Young Life was fitting into an increasingly fast-paced society that was starving for the personal touch. This formation of friendships, this contact work that they were doing, had been given them to fill a great void in the lives of people.

"We began to fill it without realizing we were supplying one of the basic needs of a human being," Bill continued. "Then we began to learn that this personal caring was the key to all communication. This was discovery for us."

Only gradually did it become apparent that they were to do this caring with no strings attached. Simply because they knew these teenagers were significant to Christ, they would be out there loving them. If the teenagers liked it, great; if they didn't like it, that was all right too. "Their response had nothing to do with how we were to behave," Bill recalled. *"We were to love them regardless."*

19

FROM THE PURCHASE of their first property, Young Life had moved into a different league. No longer able to handle all the operational details out of his briefcase, Jim had transplanted both his family and the office up to Star Ranch, south of Colorado Springs. It was not exactly downtown Dallas. Whereas Maxine and others who stayed there all the time found it lonely, Jim loved to return to its isolation from his travels. He enjoyed having Star as a showplace where he could bring in church leaders and businessmen to demonstrate his vision. He was the executive director, and the log cabin in the woods was the national headquarters.

Although the secretarial work, the mailings and bookkeeping were capably handled by four staff women, it had been apparent for some time that the Campaign was getting complicated enough to need a professional manager. John Carter, a Baptist businessman, had no intention of leaving his position with Continental Oil Company when he visited the Young Life office with Roy Riviere. But he came none too soon and was hired immediately. Some said he joined the group because of Millie Cisco, an attractive staff girl who caught John's eye that first day. Later they were married.

It was not easy for John to get Jim to change his habits. The earliest stage in the financial picture was simply people who loved Jim Rayburn slipping him a contribution personally. Whether it was fifty cents at club, a $50 pledge, or a $50,000 gift to buy a ranch, people gave because they were drawn to his ministry. And Jim always made the effort to thank each one personally.

Long after John arrived and began to standardize procedures, Jim would still say, "Look, John, people will give to me better than to this general Young Life thing back in Colorado." And the staff had learned to depend on Jim to bring in the money for all of them.

Stage two was a natural progression. As the mission grew and there were more staff who needed support, it was more realistic to make each one responsible to find whatever money he or she needed—a personal deputation kind of financing.

Stage three was debated back and forth as they tried to establish a central fund to pay all staff out of headquarters. The idea was to get people to give to the mission rather than to individuals. "All we were trying to do," Carter said, "was to get people to send their money in to headquarters so we could develop a big pool that could be split up."

The fourth stage came after considerable confusion and a lot of mistakes. Bill Starr, assigned to Portland, Oregon, pioneered the concept of a local committee to underwrite and encourage its own local club program and leadership. "What we did here was to walk right between the idea of a central pool and the idea of personally designated funds, with the thought of creating a smaller pool for each local area.

"We knew Jim couldn't get the money for all of us, but I found out I couldn't do it alone either. I needed help. I remember dashing around Portland trying to line up friends, going to see pastors, visiting parents of club kids—figuring out how to broaden the base of this financial thing. I did everything wrong in the book." He discussed his objectives with one of the earliest Dallas club leaders who had started his own youth work in the Northwest. He visited board member C. Davis Weyerhaeuser, who lived in Tacoma. "Get the people together," they suggested. "Tell them your problem, and see what happens."

Most of the people who came to Bill's first meeting were familiar with the goals and methods of Young Life, but they were surprisingly unaware of the financial difficulties Bill shared with them. Asking for more than their own gifts and pledges, he tried to communicate the need for an even broader base than they would be able to provide by themselves. He wanted them to seek support from local businesses, churches, clubs, foundations, any source they could to give it a community base. And

63

he added, "A part of the money we raise will go to Young Life headquarters in Colorado Springs to meet the general, nationwide expenses of the work. It won't all stay here in Portland."

This approach opened up an hour of discussion and lifted these first committeemen into a new and exciting adventure. When the pledges and cash were all in, the newly formed Young Life Committee of Portland found it had enough to pay the salaries of all the staff members in the Northwest region, with some left over!

With each staff person on his own out in the boondocks, it was a sink-or-swim arrangement, very different from Jim's gathering everyone into the office to pray when the money ran out. Even the men who followed the Starrs in Portland felt uneasy. "We'd never done any adult work. All that was new," Tom Raley said. "I knew how to talk to kids, not grownups. Mainly I just tried to keep in touch with the men who showed an interest—played golf, ate lunch with them. It was strictly trial and error."

Another staff man, Dick Langford, confessed, "I was disappointed because I thought the committee was going to come up with all the ideas, but they didn't know what they were supposed to do either."

When adults were able to visit a camp or local club, they were often drawn to participate because they were personally sold on what was happening. Chub Andrews, a doctor in Memphis, and his wife, Marge, were so touched by the love of Christ through Jim, that they took groups of adults along with them to visit the ranches in Colorado. For thirteen years they hauled mothers and dads back and forth so that their friends' hearts could be touched by God as their own had been. Out of this generous involvement, the Memphis Committee grew. And out of that group came the idea of having a national convention for committee people right at Frontier Ranch. This gave adults some of the same fun that the campers loved, and it provided them a firsthand appreciation of the ministry they were supporting. "Our whole committee is made up of people who've experienced Young Life in their own lives," Marge Andrews said. "They know what the Lord can do."

64

When a committee catches the vision it will create the base of fellowship a leader needs. The members become the team through whom he can gain strength and power to go out and minister. With them he is no longer alone. "But there's even more we've found out," Starr explained. "It finally came to us that we as leaders weren't ever supposed to do it all alone. We were there as a catalyst to bring other adults into usefulness in their community. They were there not only to help me, but to do things I could never do. And in the doing, their lives become richer. The use of many talents, many skills in the committee to undergird the work with kids is a concept that has broadened the whole mission."

20

THERE'S A nineteenth century story about Dwight L. Moody and his ten-acre farm in Connecticut that Ted Benson told to help people understand Rayburn. Moody asked a neighboring farmer to plow his field, but he insisted that the hired man use four horses instead of two, as he'd seen done on the big western ranches. The poor farmer almost went crazy trying to turn four horses around in that little field.

That was the way Moody thought—in terms of four horses, rather than one or two like the rest of us. Rayburn did too. He was an engineer, a four-horse plowman. After he died, his son found "Think Big" scribbled and left in pockets and drawers and books as reminders. Making large petitions was a kind of real-life game that Jim played well. He expected God to do his work in keeping with his omnipotence.

One friend tells of a train trip with Jim where they were assigned berths 13 and 14. As they walked through the Pullman, they realized that the numbers only went up to 12. So what happened? Jim pushed open a door at the end of the car and grinned, "Well, wouldn't you know? He gave us the drawing room!" Either it didn't occur to him to think of failure, or whatever sense of doubt lurked in his secret heart was dispelled by his basic desire to be in league with the Almighty.

When the Young Life family first got wind that Jim was off in the wilds of Canada looking at a *fourth* campsite, their ability to think big was stretched almost to the breaking point. But it wasn't long until they realized God was in this too. The Malibu Club had been built lavishly as an escape for Hollywood stars, perched on primordial rock jutting into the fiordlike waters of an inland waterway. A hundred miles beyond the Canadian border, lost in the pine-forested mountains, it was known chiefly to lumbermen and occasional wealthy West Coast yachters. The fact that it was reachable only by water drew protests from some of the board: "Boats are just not safe!" To which Jim drawled, "Well, I'm sure glad the Alaska Steamship Company never found that out."

As Bill Starr walked over the property with Jim, he was overwhelmed to realize that "Jim was already speaking as though it was an accomplished fact that Malibu was ours. And I thought we'd just flown up to take a look at it." It was not only the most awesome scenery they had ever seen, it was completely furnished to the last bedspread and teaspoon. They were bowled over by the possibilities it offered for Young Life, but unaware of God's greater plan. For in the acquisition of Malibu they were pushed into what would become an international dimension. In order to own property in Canada, it was necessary to form a Canadian corporation to hold Malibu in trust, so they set up Young Life of Canada for that purpose in 1954. "We never planned to be an international mission," Starr explained. "Here was another point where I can look back and see God leading, even though at the time we did not understand."

A second thing Malibu did was to open up a wider understanding of their camping philosophy. "We'd been flirting with it ever since we got Star, then Silver Cliff, then Frontier," Starr continued, "but we'd never really defined it. When we got Malibu, we had to face completely the fact that we were operating on a *resort* concept—which at that time was a very new and daring way to go in the Christian community.

66

"For one thing, we were putting fellows and girls of high school age together in the same camp, which meant we had to upgrade the facilities in all the other properties to accommodate both boys and girls at once. For this purpose Malibu was natural. It was built with facilities for both men and women, so we fell into that without even thinking about it.

"It also led us into something unique for middle-class kids who no longer wanted simply to 'go to camp.' They responded to being able to do things like the older folks did on vacation— things like lying beside the pool and sunning and talking, eating good meals in pleasant surroundings, having a pool table or a golf course to enjoy.

"The most common expression I heard at Malibu as adults would come in off their yachts was, 'Why, this is too nice for kids. This ought to be for adults.' That was a real key to turn our thinking more than ever toward three factors that we had never fully understood before."

One was *isolation*. They took kids out of their own environment, unplugged them from the radio in the ear and the TV, removed them from the struggles with family and school, the competitive strain, the daily humdrum sameness. For one week they were transported into an environment re-created just for them. For one week they were transported into a little microcosm of the kingdom of God. It was made up primarily of two highly valued components—the understanding high school Christians on the *work crew*, and the *counselors* who really sought to be this "incarnational" friend. Both of these groups working together left little doubt in a camper's mind that somebody really cared.

Number two was *adventure*. They would try to find whatever was distinctive to the location. In Colorado it was not only mountain climbing but snow sliding. Jim had scared them to death the first time he took them up on a high ridge and walked out onto a ledge of snow and disappeared. What he searched for was exactly the right place to make a drop onto an inclined snow field from which you could slide on down the slope a couple thousand feet. At Malibu it was the combination of the water, mirroring snow peaks, that made water skiing a unique experience. At Silver Cliff who could ever forget swimming

68

in water as hot as the shower at home, especially if it was snowing at the same time! Later at Castaway Club on a Minnesota lake they built a seventy-foot slide where kids would sail off twenty feet into the air before they ever hit the water. Sailboats, canoes, Hondas, moonballs, parachutes stretch teenagers to take on challenges they'd never try otherwise. Then switching as the culture dictated new edges of adventure, the camp counselors sought never to let one kind of activity get so old it lost its excitement.

There were times when danger lurked very close to adventure in far-off Malibu, where the only link to the rest of the world was a minimal short-wave radio. One day while Mitch and Starr were up above the waterfront moving furniture around in Sitka Lodge to accommodate more campers, they heard a yell, "Help! Help! Help!" Racing to the window, they saw a camper trying to pass a swim test, but almost ready to drown right there in the inlet. Previous camping experience in Colorado didn't exactly

Bill Starr helps Malibu skier

prepare them for all the hazards of thirty fathoms of water. By the time they got to the dock one of the other kids had leaped in a rowboat and was pulling the swimmer out of the water just in the nick of time. "Knock off these stupid tests!" Mitch called. "There's got to be a better way."

He and Starr were two shaky men. It was a constant effort to plan excitingly but to keep anticipating those activities that could be irreversibly dangerous.

Adventure led to the number three factor, *discovery*. Bill noted the wonder with which kids responded when they could find out new things for themselves instead of having everything pointed out to them. "We saw them discovering new aspects of themselves, new dimensions to life, new expressions of God— in Christ and in the marvels of his handiwork all about them." One girl, hiking through the Alpine meadows, exclaimed, "We don't have the teensiest chance against God out here! You guys have got it rigged."

The thing they were learning most through the camping was that the message of the gospel was not so much to be imposed on the kids as discovered. It was a privilege the counselor laid out before them, not shoved down them.

21

STAFF PEOPLE began to lean heavily on the camps. It was expected that everybody would meet the Lord at camp. "It was like a machine," Mitch said. "We fed kids in and they'd come out Christian." There was a reason, but they hadn't comprehended what it was.

"Jim had given us verses about the 'outsiders'—phenomenal verses nobody had ever pointed out before, in seminary or any other place," Bill said. "Where did anybody ever hear *'Don't judge the outsider'* . . . or *'Walk in wisdom to them who are*

without' . . . or *'I sat where they sat'*? Those were key concepts that guided us. But we didn't know very much about how to *do* these things."

Then some of the great practices which Jim had introduced began to have meaning. His taking kids up Chimney Rock was one example. Jim sat at one particular spot that always frightened kids, and he would help them over it. Instinctively he acted out what he knew was good for them. All of the counselors copied him. They learned to lead that climb, to sit in that spot, to reach out a hand to help a scared kid up the steep rock. And in the experience of leading kids over the dangerous spot every one of these big men felt like a little kid scared to death. In entering into the kids' fear, and in caring enough to do what was good for them, they began to perceive real ongoing "incarnation."

It worked equally well for the leader to put himself in a situation where he could be laughed at—especially if he was the one who was also doing the proclaiming of the gospel. When the speaker was up front early in the meeting having a lot of fun, causing a lot of laughs, it seemed to free up the kids to hear what he would say later during the message. "We didn't know how exactly," Starr said, "but again there was truth coming through."

It was the relational contact added to the program activities that made the speaking so meaningful. In sharing the kids' fears—and laughter—the idea took shape that program was not limited to events. It was everything that goes on between people at camp.

Most of the staff still thought of the Incarnation as an act of history in which Jesus Christ became a human, but gradually they were being shown that in a Christlike life there is ongoing incarnation. In the everyday encounters between persons, there are continually new, up-to-date experiences with Christ.

"We believed that Christians were meant to have fun," Mitch said, "and we were gonna show these kids one heck of a good time. We would get together and pray before we'd do any kind of entertainment. It was well-thought-out, well-rehearsed, really 'pro' stuff that we spent hours working through. In those days, entertainment was a key thing in proclaiming the gospel. It was a spiritual matter."

The idea of fun became very important in Young Life's incarnational understanding of evangelism. Bill and Mitch and Raley and Riviere tried to tailor the program so that the whole camp would participate even on those difficult mountain climbs. They would take as many as two hundred and fifty kids on a climb. Everybody went for the experience and the fun of it.

Even a crippled black girl on crutches was thrilled to be a part of the big hike at Frontier. While Bill was organizing an expedition to the Continental Divide, he saw the girl's disappointment. She could not climb. Of course, she would be left behind, conscious of her disability, maybe wondering what she had done to merit such discrimination on the part of God. Bill summoned some of the biggest, strongest boys among the teenagers and some of the sturdiest of the camp counselors. A dozen of them had been football players, and they looked the part.

Then he announced, "Fellas, Kathie's going with us. She'll need you to carry her over the rough spots and up the steep hills. Okay, Kathie?"

The disbelief, the wild happiness that leaped inside her made all of them grin as they set out with Kathie on their shoulders.

Hours later, as they rested on a hillside, Kathie said to Bill, "Nobody knows how I prayed and prayed in my heart to come along!"

22

As INTERNATIONAL students started coming to Malibu and American Field Service students began turning up at Frontier, some of the leaders became aware of a quiet, subtle influence guiding their thinking. Many of these international students were from Catholic families, and the Young Life people hadn't been around many Catholics before. The more contact they had with them, the more it dawned on them that being Christian has nothing to do with being Protestant or Catholic. It should have been obvious before; but they had never stopped to think that the message they were proclaiming was not a Protestant one— it was a biblical message they were concerned about proclaiming.

As this "cross-ecclesiastical" effect began to sift through the camps and back into the local clubs, most leaders were no longer content to limit themselves to being a Protestant mission, but set their sights on becoming truly *Christian*. The transformation was gradual and was expressed not in a change of message but in a change of attitude. They saw that they were to relate, not to one church, but to many; not to be open to just the "right" kind, but to be open to the Spirit of God leading them to all kinds. As their minds were broadened, they were willing to accept the fact that God is really bigger than any one of us, or all of us put together.

23

THE TIME was not too far off when the Young Life family would be stretched—not only to relate to foreign students and Catholics, but to take on an entirely new crosscultural experience with black young people. It would require several efforts—and a surplus of patience, courage and resilience—before it would be able to survive.

Up to this time the only black faces regularly seen around the camps were those of Andrew and Jerry Delaney, who left Philadelphia in 1951 to become the chefs at Frontier Ranch. Known to thousands of hungry kids across America, "Goldbrick" and his wife faithfully served the camps and the mission for twenty-five years before building their own restaurant in Colorado.

A few black campers who came to Frontier had a different effect—not on the kids or the staff, but on some Mississippi parents a thousand miles away. Wally Howard, Southern Director during the mid-50s, remembers the painful break with very close dear friends, people who were Christian, but who could not feel right about putting whites and blacks together. "They didn't want to tell us what to do in other parts of the country," Wally recalls, "but when their kids went to Frontier, they wanted a guarantee that there would be no black campers there. And second, they wanted a guarantee that there would be no pictures or stories about blacks in any Young Life publications."

Young Life, on the other hand, could not feel right telling young black people they were not wanted at camp because they weren't white. Reluctantly, they pulled John Miller out of Leland, Mississippi, since it seemed no longer feasible to work within the social structure that existed there at that time.

In Dallas an effort was aborted in a different way. A couple of seminary students attempted to cross the color line and estab-

*Street scuffle
with Milliken*

lish a club at one of the black high schools. It didn't work there,
at that time, to have white leaders in that position. They were
resented, and one night one of the fellows got cut up badly on
the way to club. They heeded the warning, realizing the time
was not right.

Six gang members from Newark, New Jersey, finally became
the seed for the urban effort. Harv Oostdyk had persuaded them
to leave the city streets for a "free spree" in the Rocky Mountains. At Frontier Ranch they met a young work crew rebel from
Pittsburgh who followed them everywhere. This zany Bill Milliken had thrown a dare out to God the summer before when he
too had been persuaded to attend a Young Life camp: "Christ,
if you're real, you better do something in my life 'cause I sure
need it!"

It was the wild dreaming of Oostdyk and the Milliken kid
around the "Newark Six" that made the first dent in New York
City. At age twenty, Milliken dribbled a basketball across George
Washington Bridge and into an intense, bizarre decade that
embraced Selma and Harlem, the murder of Martin Luther
King, and the rise of a new Afro-American dignity. Oostdyk and
Milliken together pioneered in the streets and the parks, in
Harlem and the Lower East Side. They found occasional support
from a brave clergyman, a wealthy corporation executive, a
prophetic government representative. Through shock, rejection,
doubt, despair, even mental breakdown, they refused to be
knocked out. They opened apartments for tough guys and girls

who had never known what it meant to have a home where they felt loved. They established street academies to prove to the world that blacks and browns were not stupid, but could learn anything if their minds and imaginations were released in an environment of genuine concern. They held clubs; set up week-end outings; went to court; dealt with sex in every form; collected money for bail, for bad teeth, for broken bones; and learned to cut through miles of red tape. The Christian aspects of Young Life, which Milliken tried to discuss with them, were put to every test imaginable. For years, these kids had resisted all efforts of churches to get to them.

On the 2,000-mile station-wagon trip to Frontier, Bill didn't mind their loud, profane exuberance. They sang as if they were yelling. They shouted and whistled at girls as they passed through towns. All this Milliken identified with—just the normal high-spirits of teenagers on vacation. What did disturb him was the discovery that his group was stealing items on overnight motel stops—towels, ashtrays, and other small things—for the sheer thrill of getting away with it. He tried to lecture them, but further learned that some of them were even getting out of restaurants free after devouring complete steak dinners.

At Frontier, they were a small minority among two hundred other teenagers, including many blacks, so they had to behave. The rest of the campers would not put up with their horsing around. That became clear early in the week, as they refused to allow interruptions of club talks or Bible discussions or prayer. The New Yorkers sat through most of the sessions in silence, but some of them never discarded their smirks as they listened to talks about Christ's love for all people.

Toward the end of the week, Milliken felt his effort had been futile. His New York men, so far as he could see, showed no interest in Jesus, no inclination to try a new future under his power and authority. Milliken had counted on some of them to back him up among their friends at home, helping him maybe even to form a club. Watching the group as they listened to the words of Bill Starr or Bob Mitchell, he lost hope.

The evening before they were to start home, Milliken went to the cabin he shared with his six charges. He did not expect to find anyone in the dark room. But the door was open, and on the threshold Milliken stopped.

One of his New Yorkers was alone in the cabin. In hoarse tones that blended anguish with defiance, he was saying, "If *you* can do anything with this life, Jesus, go ahead and do it. I'm messed up. I don't have no place to go. I hate my father. I hate my mother. I even hate myself. Please, for God's sake, if there's anything You can do, *do it!*"

No matter what happened now, Milliken knew his attempt had been blessed. His dare with God had held after all, and this cry in the dark cabin would not go unheard.

24

THE ENTRY INTO urban communities was a dangerous challenge. "In recent years," Starr said, "the city cores have confronted us with problems we never knew existed. Amid the poverty and

Oostdyk leads early urban club. Milliken, right of center.

hopelessness of thousands of families we have seen the effect of hard-core unemployment, teenage drug addiction, crime, illiteracy, prostitution, gang violence, and countless other social evils. What possible good could it do here to form the kind of club we'd been running in the pleasant suburbs of Los Angeles or Philadelphia?

"These kids desperately needed Christ," he went on, "but what they thought they needed more than anything else was money, medicine, food, a job, a home. They needed someone to hold onto as they withdrew from drugs, someone to go with them to court or to get them out of jail. They had to be literally hauled out of bed every morning once they had been tutored into prep school. Girls, some of them not yet fourteen, had to be taken off the streets where they worked for pimps. There was a mighty day-to-day, hour-to-hour job to be done, such as we in Young Life had never before faced. Men like George Sheffer convinced us of that and were also willing to lead the way."

Without knowing where to turn for city-bred leaders, Young Life had to puzzle over how this new breed of men kept emerging—men like Oostdyk, Jabo Cox, Vince Pasquale—tough alumni of ghetto environments. Most youngsters in the city had to be approached on street corners, in parks, doorways, pool parlors, bars, and similar hangouts. It was no job for women; but a few insisted on being present anyway and were impossible to turn away. Mary Miller brought her Master's in Sociology to the streets of New York; Joan Thompson moved out of the western suburbs into Chicago's heart. Both stayed to marry black men and become strong centers of God's love. It was not a safe job for anyone. Two Young Life men in Chicago were brutally beaten. After three weeks in a coma, Joan's husband died.

Always the urban staff sought new approaches to meet practical inner-city needs. Classes were started in Harlem's Church of the Master. They called it an Academy of Transition in the hope of helping kids who could scarcely read to bridge the gulf between street learning and books. They started where the kids were, with the then-popular *Autobiography of Malcolm X*. In a number of cases the effort caught hold. Kids who were curious enough to inquire found a place where they could come for

79

Bobo Nixon, one-time gang leader, directs his own mission to New York street kids.

assistance in almost anything. School dropouts resumed their education. Drug addicts kicked their habits. Gang members found decent jobs. Other Academies opened in storefronts, manned by Young Life's urban pioneers. They had to be free-wheeling personalities who were willing to ride bicycles through Manhattan traffic, and could flex with almost everything.

Their undertaking was financed principally by gifts from interested New Yorkers and New York corporations. No one could dispute the value of guiding kids off the street into the paths of useful citizenship. Oostdyk and Milliken were both mysterious and effective in their appeal to philanthropists on Wall Street as well as junkies in the subway. At any rate, money kept coming from unexpected places. Giving to urban renewal was the "in" thing in the U.S. of the mid '60s.

About the same time a white man in Florida chose to work unnoticed with the poor whites. Jabo Cox was not at all like the white guys in New York. He had left home before he was a teenager; and the circus, the Navy, the city had all been his school. He had bummed around the world, supported a $100-a-day drug habit, been a male prostitute, driven a bus and a truck, and owned (and lost) his own service station.

It wasn't easy for Jabo to accept the blacks in Young Life, but it was even harder for him to accept the white "jocks." His first impression after driving a busload of kids from Knoxville, Tennessee, to Colorado was simply, "I don't know what you people got, but I hope to God I never catch it!" Young Life didn't know what to do with him; and he sure didn't know what to do with them. But for better or worse, they seemed to be stuck with each other.

80

Jabo and Jacksonville friends

Jabo became a familiar figure on the streets of Jacksonville and then Orlando. The kids in his clubs have been abused, neglected, and unloved—kids who are so badly damaged that Jabo knows their only hope is in the strength and love of Jesus Christ. He knows that because of his own experience. "I met the Lord because of a follower, not a leader," he says. "And I realized if I was gonna follow Christ, I was gonna have to let the needle and all that stuff go."

The poor whites in the city got lost as the black movement got rolling. Nobody was saying "Poor white's beautiful," but Jabo, hanging out on his corner, gave them something to belong to. It didn't make any difference if a guy had a record or if a girl was pregnant; they could hang out at Young Life and belong. One girl told him, "It just seems to be only one hour a week that I feel like a human being. That's when I'm sittin' in that club and some of the crap on the streets just sort of disappears. At least I'm away from it for an hour where we can sing and see a stupid skit and hear someone talk about Somebody that cares . . . not only talkin' about Somebody who cares, but the guy doin' the talkin', carin'."

She was saying the same thing Bill Starr was saying about the incarnation. God had come to her turf in the shape of Jabo Cox. Some of Jabo's kids had never known anyone who could say, "I care, you know." It blows their minds when he says, "Here I am. I don't work with the state. I'm not a caseworker. I'm not here to write a book. I'm just here."

25

BACK IN Colorado Springs, a troubled Board of Directors met to discuss the delicate social issue presented by the urban experiment. *Had Young Life been organized to combat social evils? Or was its real function to bring young people to a belief in Jesus Christ?*

There were now members on the board who came from large cities with urban problems; people like W. Robert Stover, president of Western Temporary Services in San Francisco; Marvin D. Heaps, president of ARA Food Services in Philadelphia; Dr. William Kiesewetter of the Children's Hospital in Pittsburgh; and others who understood urban needs. Even they were divided in their opinions.

One man would argue, "The cities have dozens of social agencies that are working on all these problems. Why do we have to duplicate what is already being done?"

Another pleaded, "It's too dangerous. Let's stop before it's too late. It's pretty clear we're not wanted."

A third had searched all through Young Life's constitution. "I don't see a single line where it says we've got to become a job placement bureau for delinquents and addicts. Besides, we're not getting anywhere."

But there were others who had convictions that the disadvantaged teenagers of the cities needed Christ as much as the fortunate kids of the middle-class suburbs, and they were not ready to abandon their commitment to them.

Young Life could no longer be a suburban subculture. It was being pressed to explode beyond the theological systems into the acute suffering of a hostile world. The Savior, who had become real in the lives of so many high school leaders throughout the past two and a half decades, was affirming his availability to all kids everywhere.

26

BRANCHING OUT into the city turned everything around in Young Life. Damage in life, processed by God's Spirit, became value. Pain became growth. Failure became understanding. And what looked like success could crumble by sundown.

"We've been so conditioned to think that things fall apart when we're honest," Milliken said. "We don't want a crisis. We don't want pain. We don't want suffering. But we were discovering that it's through these things that we grow up. It may be just in saying to a friend, 'What are you going to do about that?' that he, or she, can become beautiful. Unless someone is challenging us to look at ourselves, to make us go deeper, we will always stop short of our potential."

In perceiving the importance of caring for each other, the fellowship was coming of age. They began to recognize evangelism as a corporate matter, beyond the primary thrust of salvation into a person's life. There also was a deepening recognition that God was calling a group of people in a local community to bring change into the entire community, not only to high school kids. There was a growing commitment to one another in order to accomplish God's will on earth, as it is in heaven.

"When that happens," said Bob Reeverts, who joined the staff in 1961 directly out of Fuller Seminary, "my commitment to a man on my staff means I'm going to be driven to be concerned about his family, the next two or three decades of his life. I can't only have in mind, 'How's your club going today?' I take a real interest in his growth in all areas of his life. These were things that were driving us together."

Through the medley of success and failure, the city was performing a prophetic function for the entire staff, and God was proving again that he would not let go. In the midst of an inhuman milieu at the great cities' heart, he was demonstrating that he holds the key to unlocking human potential everywhere. He was confronting them with life-changing demands.

Some were convinced that the ultimate solution for the city lay within the city itself—not in the outside leaders, but in the young people who grew up in the streets. One of the principles was to get their young disciples out of the ghetto to gain new perspectives, then get them back into the city to build on these new strengths. The finding and refining of indigenous leadership, they believed, would save the ghetto. It was a deep and meaningful commitment to Christ on the part of individuals, linked to revolutionary social change, that would carry hope for the city's future. What emerged more slowly was the fact that this same quality of commitment to revolutionary change was a basic requirement for the ongoing direction of the entire mission—not only the city.

After twenty years of focusing on the scrubbed and polished, cheer-leading, fashion-clad segment of adolescent society, Young Life was widening its scope dramatically. As the campaigners faced into the prejudice of racism, they also bumped into barriers in their own personal encounters. In their commitment to plunge ahead they were often clumsy. They were zealous. They were stubborn. They were blunt. And in the long, slow process some were badly bruised.

In the '60s, as in the '40s, there were no pat formulas, no timetables, no blueprints.

The unmistakable hand of God had led Young Life into some undeniable ways to relate to adolescents anywhere. What Milli-

Pittsburgh urban team

ken was doing in New York, Jabo was doing in Jacksonville—
and Rayburn had done in Gainesville. It was an attitude that
could be implemented a thousand ways—that *disinterested teenagers are important enough to merit Special Handling.* The camp
properties, the club program, the personal friendship—all said
so. The quality of attention affirmed the worth of the individual and opened the door to new possibilities. It recognized the
young person's need to be taken seriously.

The expansion of this proven principle was now calling some
of the leadership to a larger context. It was not only the young
person who was important enough to merit special handling.
It was his mother. His father. It was not only the club *kid,* it was
also the club *leader.* It was not only the old call to "walk in
wisdom to those who are without," but it was a call to "love
one another." In the city. In the suburbs. In the staff meeting.
In the family circle. And beyond.

27

FROM THE SMALL beginning with American Foreign Service
students visiting Frontier and Malibu, Jim was coaxed into looking at South America by a young West Coast staff man. Ron
Frase had asked the Presbyterian Church to send him to Brazil,
but frustration hounded him when he could find no one who
knew how to interest young Brazilians in Jesus Christ. A letter to
Young Life met with favorable response. Jim saw every reason
why the same respect they showed kids in North America would
work just as well south of the border.

Step one was a survey trip by Mitch and his wife Claudia to
look over the possibilities. They returned to report that "the
people are beautiful, and the Presbyterian Church down there
wants us."

The Advisory Committee looked around for the right man to pioneer in Brazil and stopped with Harry MacDonald, a self-starter and a trouble-shooter. His clubs in Pittsburgh were already being handled by Reid Carpenter while Harry was studying at L'Abri, an experimental theological center in Switzerland.

"We all agreed on Harry," said Bill Starr. "He had pulled off more stuff than anyone in his seventeen years on staff with his creativity, his adaptability and hustle. We were really trying to evaluate people's gifts in this case—something I can't recall doing before—and Harry was our man."

"I didn't want to go at all," Harry countered. "We'd already been away a year, and the kids were ready to start high school. Besides, I'd flunked Spanish, and South America had absolutely no appeal for me. I thought, If this is a political move, count me out." By the time the five MacDonalds were aboard ship for Sao Paulo, they figured it was not political, it was God.

What Harry demonstrated during his five years in Brazil was the same idea Rayburn and Starr had discussed three years earlier during a trip to Europe. Harry found out he could give the Young Life message and methods to the Brazilians who wanted it. That was the secret. *If the Brazilians wanted it, then they would utilize it in their own culture.*

In 1959, Jim had wanted a first-class international experience for his top twelve men. He wanted them in tuxedos. He wanted them to know the right fork to pick up. He wanted them to be introduced to the right wines with their meals. He took them to Europe, and it was an adventure in excellence all the way. But there was more to it than that—

One night in a German hotel, Rayburn and Starr dined with John O'Neill, who had started a club there among the American military high school students. As they ate their meal, John was saying, "It's great going to these American kids, but what we ought to do is get to the Germans!" And Jim in his mellow way asked, "And how are we to go to the Germans?" "That's no problem," O'Neill fired back. "Let the Germans come to us." As the conversation continued, someone remarked, "Wouldn't it be wonderful if instead of our going all over the world, God would send people from all over the world to us?" "That's it!" Jim said.

A number of Europeans made an impact on Jim that trip, but it was the impact his blonde daughter made on a handsome German that God was going to use to work out that give-it-away concept in at least one foreign culture. Diether Koerner not only followed Sue Rayburn all the way back to Coloraro Springs, but he stayed long enough to get converted. And several years later he took all he had learned about God, and about Young Life, to share with high school kids in the Peruvian culture.

Almost a decade after that meeting in the German hotel, Harry MacDonald was named International Coordinator for Young Life. It was 1971, and all that had been learned about crosscultural experience in countless situations with teenagers now contributed to the development of the new philosophy— to give the message away and let it be used as it best fits the new culture. What they know for sure is that their message transcends culture, that Jesus Christ is for everyone. What they also know is that the life of God in a human being draws kids to Christ as a leader spends time *with* them—and that this principle of "with-ness" works as well in Hong Kong as it does in Atlanta.

When Harry and Hope MacDonald first went to Brazil, the thing that was most attractive to the young Brazilians was their family life. They had seen no model like it before. They had never seen a man treat his wife as Harry treated Hope, or the way Harry and Hope treated their children, or the way the children fit into the family with their parents. One girl said to them, "Why do you think we come to your house? We don't see love like this other places."

Hal Merwald, who followed Harry in Brazil, asked the high school coach in Campinas if he could run on the local track to keep in shape. Some of the schools were also using the track for physical education classes, and a few students began to run along with him. One day the coach commented, "I used to think this American was running around there just like any other man for exercise. Then one day he brought his two-year-old son to run with him, and the way he treated his child, and the way they ran together . . . no Brazilian has ever seen this! No Brazilian ever treats his son that way." This small act unlocked the whole high school to Hal and the young nationals working with him.

Hal explains, "This fruit of the Spirit that I believe the incarnational Christ gives to us is what actually attracts. We can use external things like a coffee house, or playing pool, or a youth center, or a club, or a camp; but the real key is what Christ does that makes this life attractive. When a young person is attracted to a quality of life, he cannot resist observing and inquiring about this person, who can then take him across the bridge to the Person Jesus Christ."

It's as simple as it can be: here is this culture, and here are these people existing in it. Then all of a sudden here comes a person who is very attractive because he or she demonstrates qualities that are the fruit of Christ's love. It's a light, a beacon that attracts.

Left, Harry McDonald; right, Bruce Sunberg

Kim Jong Dal, visiting in the United States, lived several months in the St. Louis home of Young Life leader Bruce Sundberg. Kim is highly respected in South Korea and has many contacts there. What he saw in Bruce's life made such an impact on him that he returned to Seoul and started several Young Life clubs to reach Korean young people for Christ. Kim described what he saw in Bruce: "His action and his thinking is equal . . . most men speak wonderful but action is different. In the world, Christian is wonderful speak, but living style is very bad. I saw Bruce speak and living equal. He is wonderful man and my friend."

One by one new countries quietly join the Young Life family. Each time it is an unheralded slipping into the local culture at some personal point of entry. A California minister moves his family to Austria. A missionary couple in France begins to notice the problems of young people through their maturing children. A businessman opens his home to Bermuda teenagers. "When we come into a new culture," Merwald says, "previous structures are up for grabs. As we are incarnational with those people, then God will let us know what programs we ought to create and what tools we ought to use. Then we can go from there. And it's not only at the beginning this must happen, but all along the way too. We've got to be willing to say, 'It's not working; let's try something else.' "

From the early Texas days, Jim had always taught his people to critique and evaluate what they did to see if it was working. Driving home from the Ft. Worth club thirty years prior to Merwald's comment, Jim would say, "What did you think about tonight?" Sometimes it was good; other times it was very bad. It was always: Keep the good. Throw out the bad. What do we want to change? What is worth doing again? How can we improve it?

Annie Cheairs, who spent the first half of her life working with Jim and the staff, said, "I'm so grateful that I have the willingness to try something. And that even if it fails, I don't have to feel like I'm a failure. It's ingrained in me—the ability to try something and see what happens. The keen sense of humor that was so woven through our history has given us this freedom to experiment. If we did something good, it was marvelous. If it doesn't come off well, we accept it and later it becomes a hilarious story, or it turns up somewhere in a skit." After almost thirty years on staff, Annie—as if testing her own philosophy— left for Africa as a short-term missionary.

28

THE WINDS OF change were blowing in several directions. Some of the staff had stayed in the same place long enough to meet their failures coming down the street and were starting to ask

89

why. What was happening to those kids who went through the Young Life system and had no significant, lasting change in their lives? Many were looking for ongoing help for their club kids— a follow-up procedure that would nurture the life of God inside them.

For a long time "Campaigners" had been a place for kids who met Christ and then wanted to know how to follow Him in their everyday living. "That's my favorite part," said Gail Grimston, one of the Canadian staff. "I love opening the Scriptures with kids, ministering to the total person, getting to deal with them where they struggle. I think about one girl who was so sick at one of our weekend camps that she had to leave early to see the doctor. She discovered she had viral bronchitis, which meant she had to give up being in a very important crew race. Then she also told me her parents had been in Florida for five months, and the first day she went back to school after she was sick, her car was stolen. How did she deal with all of this at once? It was tremendous to watch her wrestle with it. 'I'd be really upset,' she told me, 'if I didn't know that Jesus Christ cared about me. Sometimes I don't understand what that means, but what I do know is that my life is no longer centered around the fact that I can't be in a crew race because I'm sick, or that my car is stolen.' "

Some of the leaders themselves were struggling with disappointments in their own lives and conflicts in their families. A few were downright discontented.

From the era of the all-night prayer meeting to the newest trend of the sensitivity group was a painful leap for some; for others it was salvation. People who carried heavy personal loads into those prayer sessions had found it difficult to pray without resolving the thing that was looming between them and someone else in the group. One man had gone to Jim and said, "I can't go on praying with this anger I have against my brother." Jim responded, "We can't talk about that now; we're praying about the mission." To the man in distress it was an absolute denial of his problem. He simply could not stand the burden of being phony among his own staff people.

Before Wally Howard resigned in 1959, he and his wife,

Esther, made an effort to get help for the staff in the area of interpersonal relationships. As Dean of the Young Life Institute, a required training experience for staff, Wally had invited Dorothy Jayne to be a kind of resident counselor for one month. Mrs. Jayne came to Colorado from her private counseling practice. She met one-to-one with the students who needed someone to talk with. She also got staff people into group situations in which she devised structured ways of being human, sharing weaknesses as well as strengths. In earlier years there had been psychologists at the Institute, but they had lectured on the dynamics between adolescents and adults rather than giving actual practice in relating. At Mrs. Jayne's suggestion, the Philadelphia team even hired a psychiatrist the next year to meet an hour a week with them.

Things began to open up as the staff started to integrate their theology with a study of their own behavior. After the Howards moved over to their new posts with Faith At Work, they were invited back to Colorado to lead the College Prep Camp during the summer of 1963. "We got the kids into small groups," Esther remembered, "talking about what they were feeling, what they were afraid of, what they would like to have happen. We did a presentation to prepare them; then we let them talk with each other. The kids loved it."

At a weekend camp in the Los Angeles area, Tom Bade got

about sixty of his leaders together in the mountains for a similar group experience. Wally spoke on James 5:16—the need for admission of "sins to each other . . . so that . . . you may be healed." Bade came up to him afterwards to exclaim, "Wow! That's a whole new lifestyle!"

Add Sewell looked back over the years and commented, "My understanding of Jesus' relationship to the Pharisees was a judgment on them, not because they failed to do what they spoke about (they were very good at keeping the minutiae of the law), but they failed to do a couple of things. One, in their failure to practice justice and mercy, they omitted love. And two, I think Jesus was saying to them, 'You're not admitting the pain you feel . . . you're not recognizing the hurt inside you. You're continuing to say that the good things you do take care of all that.' And that's where I think we are," Add told the group. "We've got to start with the admission of our hurts where we're failing." And in later years he added, "If Jim could only have done that! Not just the headache pain. I mean the uncertainty inside, the doubt, the fear, the loneliness. . . ."

For a while some on the staff were uncomfortable with "doing psychology" instead of the gospel. They felt the two disciplines were mutually exclusive—either you did one or the other. For a few others the pendulum didn't swing far enough or fast enough. They couldn't wait for the changeover, so they left Young Life.

Jake Coss, who had met Christ in club and then gone on into psychology professionally, said, "Our Young Life goal primarily was to get converts into heaven . . . although we accidentally were doing a lot of loving, caring, supportive things in order to get kids to listen to our message. We called it 'contact' work, and justified all that kindness so they could come to club and 'get converted.' The club itself, with all the kids sitting on the floor, close together, touching, laughing, feeling open and excited to belong to the group—these are the things we therapists try hard to duplicate in order to bring healing to our clients. So I guess although the warm human interest, and the evangelism, appeared to be poles apart, they actually were not." But when we said, "Let's sit down and do these warm, accepting kinds of

things, in a structured way, on purpose, some people got threatened. Sometimes it was so threatening it got downright silly.
When the leader would say, 'Come on! You guys aren't open,'
someone like Mitch would respond, 'All right. By dingy-dongies!
We'll be open!' "

"I got into one of those early groups with Shelton, and that
was death!" Mitch started laughing just remembering. "There
was no way the group could be serious with Jimmy Shelton there,
and Bob Reeverts, and Terry Olson. This wonderful little guy
who led the group would have tears in his eyes as he talked to
us about the warmest room in his house, or whatever, and we
would just be splitting our sides. But we went through with it.
And what it did show us was something we had been overlooking.
That was that on our Young Life staff there were people who
had big needs, and that we'd better wise up to them."

Some were beginning to catch on, but young Bade was not
satisfied. For a long time he adapted and stayed where he was;
but he was determined to find out why teenagers rebel against
the accepted institutions such as the family and the church.
There were problems in his own family and other staff that
troubled him, and he suspected they were hampering the ministry
to kids as well as hurting the leaders. He traveled to Germany to
see if he could get a different perspective. When he returned, he
knew he had to do something. Finally he charged into a regional
directors' meeting like a young bull challenging the herd. Always
a skilled performer, Tom pulled several 3x5 cards from his
pocket and began reading authentic descriptions of anonymous
staff people who were heavily burdened with personal problems:
a pending divorce, a homosexual, a drinking habit, an affair, a
pregnant daughter. The room was silent, the men stunned, as
Tom declared, "I am one of those cards. Is there a place in
Young Life for me?"

Most of the men were incapable of handling his sudden display of suffering. One quoted Scripture. A newcomer tried to
open up the meeting to discussion by asking, "How are we going
to help Tom? He needs us." And a third orated, "We're in trench
warfare against the devil. If you aren't fit, get out!"

"I ask for bread and you give me stones," Bade puzzled.

Eventually Tom Bade left the staff to go into full-time counseling. But before he did, he had pioneered a new path of community and brotherly love.

"A wave of honesty was hitting the mission," Bill Starr observed, "and people were wanting to be human beings. It astounded me that Bade seemed to think he had weaknesses that maybe the rest of us didn't have. Up to that point I figured everybody had them and lived with them, and this was just part of the struggle of life. For the first time someone had the insight to state publicly that maybe there was more to being a leader than faith and spiritual solidness. What has been of lasting importance about that event is that it opened up the healthy discovery that the *humanness* of a leader is also vital to the mission."

A number of factors fed their confidence as they picked their way along the new path: the urban work; the influence of Sam Shoemaker and Faith At Work; a lot of books that began to come out about psychology and theology; the whole new program at Fuller Seminary in California which deliberately set out to integrate the two disciplines. Then there was the existential factor that arose as senior staff people became parents of their own teenagers. When "just preaching" was no longer the answer for their own children, staff moms and dads began to look around for a skilled Christian counselor who could help them face specific problems without undermining their conservative theology.

To recognize that God can work through psychology as well as through Bible study and prayer was a long stride. And the beauty was that through the turmoil the Lord preserved the fellowship and came through with greater wisdom for all who sought it from him.

29

THE THRASHINGS and confusion and fumbling continued to go on beneath the smooth, bright surface—which was what most people saw and appreciated in the clubs and camps. An entire decade had passed without the purchase of any new properties. The leaders had been whipping kids up and down the Rockies and shipping them in and out of Malibu—stretching them physically and emotionally in all kinds of healthy competition.

Phil McDonald, from the Minneapolis-St. Paul area, had put in twelve summers as program director at the ranches. "After we got into the '60s, it began to occur to us that kids were pretty revved up when they came to camp," McDonald said. "They needed unwinding. Those were explosive times in society, and kids were coming to us all steamed up about dress codes, the Vietnam war, and assassinations. We felt our task was to meet them on that level, but to kind of slow them down as the week went on. Get them communicating with each other and with God. Maybe we were overemphasizing the physical aspect of the program. We always talked about providing a place where kids could find personal relationship, but maybe it really wasn't all that personal, and we weren't relating to the extent we thought we were."

On concluding that they ought to create a more restful environment where kids could cool down, they received an unexpected offer from Winnipeg. Gordon Smith, who had served on the Young Life of Canada Board, was offering them a beautiful family estate outside Detroit Lakes, Minnesota. After fifty years of enjoying the property, he and his family felt it no longer met their needs, and in 1963 they asked Young Life if they could use it. It was to be an outright gift—fifteen acres, about six of it landscaped with lawn and flowers and trees, over-looking a beautiful lake.

"The whole business was ours," McDonald beams. "It was a great big spacious green island. And we called it 'Castaway.'"

Castaway was billed as a place to relax, a place to get away from the hassles. Rather than creating a Disneyland of action, McDonald started putting together a program where kids who came could get more in touch with themselves. "We wanted a peaceful place that would especially appeal to kids whose heads were messed up, whose minds were spinning," McDonald said. "A casual, de-programmed approach to camping seemed right for us."

Here again was a refocus; kids weren't quite the same as they had been in Rayburn's heyday. Castaway opened up a way to get to those hard-to-find kids. And McDonald's team began to look for the ones who are tough to relate to because they don't show up at the high school games or plays or dances. They don't hang out with the herd. They're not down in the parks. "More than likely they're over in somebody's basement freaking out over music," says McDonald, who appreciates music. "Some of the kids wouldn't even come to club, but our leaders are still able to do something because they're inventive in how to approach them."

Dick Lowey, for instance, is one who can talk with kids about all the different recording stars and styles of music. He can help them develop some discernment in their likes and dis-likes. He can share his own music with them—his great piano, his silly lyrics, his funny voice and hilarious faces. Here was a variation on the old Rayburn theme "Share your own enthusi-asms about life."

"If you can't talk to a kid about hockey or football in a way that makes him feel that you know what you're talking about," Phil goes on, "then don't try. Talk about what comes naturally

to you. Kids want to know just about anything if it comes out of your own discovery of life, and you're not just putting them on."

30

ON THE HEELS of Castaway—and more in line with its camping concept—Woodleaf, Windy Gap, and Saranac would eventually follow. One was a California gold mining town, one a contemporary hideaway in the Smokies, and one a fully outfitted camp in the Adirondack lake country.

In November 1963, there were other immediate requests for the Board to ponder: a seaworthy ship for proper camper transportation to Malibu, a $15,000 remodeling job for Castaway, completion of the new headquarters building in Colorado Springs . . . plus the request for nearly a half-million dollars for Trail West, the adult resort that would give families the kind of adventure their teenagers had loved for so long.

"When Jim gave his director's report," board man Robert Stover commented, "we would just sit there awestruck by the quality and imagination of the man. He was phenomenal! But as we got into the fiscal responsibility or a judgment decision on economics, we were torn apart as businessmen. There was such a gap between following Jim's leadership on the one hand, and handling the economics to keep up with him on the other. For ten years we had sat there and let Jim's leadership supersede the financial problems we had. Our respect for him and his love for the Savior was greater than our insistence that the mission be sensibly plotted from an economic perspective. Sometimes we wondered, maybe a mission doesn't have to be run like a business."

As the organization got larger and larger, this was no longer an option. It looked as though Rayburn had created something he could no longer manage. Added to his debatable fiscal choices was his increasing health problem. Ulcers piled on top of migraines until he was taking medication to get going, and medication to shut himself down. Sometimes the sleeping medicine would take no effect until twelve hours later, when it would hit him in the middle of a talk or a personal conversation. The healthy, beautiful things were undeniably existent in this unique man of God, yet there was also that human element through which it all arrived. And in that humanness there was weakness that bumbled and hurt.

An informal board meeting in San Francisco had disclosed the extent of staff complaints about Jim's condition and its effect on his performance. A large chunk of the Fall 1963 agenda would be given over to discussing the need for Rayburn to delegate authority to his regional directors. It was obvious that other men must begin to shoulder the executive load while Jim was still present to instruct them out of his experience.

Roy Riviere remembers an early morning ride with Tom Raley in which the question came up, "If you were the Lord, Roy, and you were going to pick a disciple band, who would you pick?"

"The mental model that came to mind," Roy recalled, "was that of the Green Beret forces in the Korean war. My effort would be to find a complementary group of experts: someone superb at finance because our disciple band would have to have money; some fellow superb at communication, both for what he could do, and for what he could teach the rest of us to do; and someone superb at kid-glove diplomacy, so we could keep the Sanhedrin from wiping us out. It would be a real combination of experts.

"Of course, it's patently obvious that the Lord himself almost went overboard in the opposite direction. Apparently what he was looking for in his disciple band was a totally different concept. What he seemed to be looking for was a group of men who had the capacity to learn to trust him. He was not so much interested in giving them some degree of direction for their talents, as having his vast power operating through them as channels.

"And I think the magnificence that we all picked up from Jim Rayburn was that he seriously wanted God to use him. In spite of all the things that we knew to be wrong with him, there was one thing that came through even more than that. It wasn't an ego-trip, even though he had a king-sized ego. It was a love affair with the Savior."

31

BLISTERING CHARGES of undermining church youth work had been hurled at Young Life from several major denominations in the earlier days. Church publications had called them "irreverent," "shameful shams," "harmful to the minds of youth." One went so far as to say "they capitalize on the ignorance of their supporters by exploiting to the highest degree a type of theology that faded into oblivion long ago."

The criticism always caught Jim full blast. It was an utter rejection of him as a man, as well as of his ministry, and it played a significant role in his life. "Jim didn't mean to be blasphemous or irreverent," Maxine explained. "He just saw the church as a colossal failure. He didn't mean for individuals to take this personally. He wanted Christians everywhere to face the reality of people being turned off to Christ . . . to care about the fact that as an organization the church was boring people. Jim didn't have any axes to grind or any big reformation to start. He just longed to see all the people who were in churches—big churches, little churches—aware of what was happening to kids . . . and praying about it, if nothing else."

Although Jim was ordained a Presbyterian, Presbytery didn't particularly like what he was doing, and didn't know what to do with him.

Complaints recurred continuously over the years. Some civic leaders labeled Young Life "communist," concluding that adults

Jim entertains
club group

who successfully gain a youth following must be suspect. Certain clergymen could see no reason for the staff to operate outside the church. Some churchmen were indignant about its nondenominational approach.

At an early staff conference, Jim had spoken out to the staff, "The church is only the church when it is more concerned about people on the outside than it is about people on the inside. I'm sorry we're so slow in filling the churches with youngsters. But one reason we're slow in winning the hearts of kids is because in the past, so many people have been abrupt and impatient with them. Don't ever try to rush a teenage kid. Don't try to push him into a decision. He'll climb off your bandwagon and run in the other direction."

Even though he felt throughout the years that he had been rejected by the church as a bona fide minister of the gospel, there was an underlying thread of desire to pass on to the larger Body of Christ what was being learned in Young Life. In the early '60s, he made a strategic move to do this. He invited Christian leaders from all over the country to join him in Chicago at the Union League Club to talk about young people and how to reach them with the love of Christ.

"The Chicago Fellowship was a remarkable idea," Bill Starr said, "whatever the motivation was. I think it was Jim's way of asking for acceptance, but it was also to help churchmen understand that Young Life was a useful tool, an authentic way to help them get the gospel out."

During the session, when one of the leaders criticized young people who would not go to church, Sam Shoemaker, Episcopalian clergyman and author, made his classic observation

102

that has been quoted so many times since, "You can't expect to put live chicks under a dead hen." Sam came from the Pittsburgh Experiment, which was pulling Christians together in the "Steel City."

Alvin Rogness came down from Luther Seminary in Minneapolis. Bishop Hubbard was there from the Episcopalian Missionary District of Spokane. Dr. John MacKay, president of Princeton Theological Seminary, came in to give the final message. Out of this one-time conference, representatives of the main denominations were to create smaller satellite fellowships. Lutherans, Methodists, Presbyterians, Baptists, Episcopalians would meet and put together their own study program out of what they gained at the Chicago Fellowship: Here's how we can reach the young people of our denomination for Christ. The strategy outlined that each local church would provide lay leaders who could be trained by the Young Life leader in the area. That would mean that the staff person would join the local church body, and this training of youth leaders would be his church work. "It was a prime idea," Mitch recalled, "if the churches could have pulled it off. Ministers on the local level were poles apart. At one local conference one minister kept nudging the man next to him, asking, 'What's that guy's name across from us?' They had both been ministering in the same town for twenty years, and they just didn't know each other."

On the other side of the fence were the problems that were gnawing away at Jim. The rejection he had experienced over the years had chewed deeply. He met with a few of the local ministers, and he would come on so positively, "There's a broad opportunity available to us. It's a golden opportunity for maximum openness to the glorious gospel of Christ. It's woven into the very fiber of being by the Creator of personality. It is the age of adolescence." He would have thirty pastors all tuned in . . . and then he would lapse and come out with something like, "This would all be great, except for a snake in the grass in a church here that is pulling us apart."

Every man there wondered if Rayburn was referring to him, and the whole conference would turn to ice. In Berkeley, Colorado Springs, Lincoln, he lashed out and ruined the chance to be heard. It was a blind area in him. He could not stand the hurt he felt from being rejected as a minister of the gospel.

Not long afterward, in a leading Methodist church, five hundred people had gathered for a training meeting where Rayburn was to speak. Bill Starr and Roy Riviere had accompanied him on the trip. At the hotel he told them to go ahead and he would meet them at the church. Jim was a little late in arriving, but the pastor gave him a warm-hearted introduction. Then he got up to speak, and it was evident that something was wrong. He stumbled as he went to the lectern. His face was gray. He tried to talk but could only mumble incoherently. He squeezed his eyes shut as if to clear his brain. That changed nothing. The words would not come.

As he swayed and almost fell, Roy stepped forward and took his arm, apologizing to the congregation for the obvious fact that Mr. Rayburn would not be able to give his message. The church sat in utter silence. In his mortification, Jim began to weep as Roy and Bill helped him to a seat. And Roy stepped to the platform to speak as best he could, in an effort to preserve the dignity of the man they had followed for almost twenty years.

Until then, no one had been willing to suggest that Jim be replaced as chief executive officer of Young Life. He and the mission he had founded seemed inseparable. His early leadership had been brilliant and far-sighted. Even when he had rammed camp projects through a dubious board, the directors eventually knew they were right to yield to his enthusiasms.

Things changed after that day Jim so helplessly left the platform in a faraway church. Many of his friends on the board and staff were forced to recognize that Jim Rayburn was no longer the energetic, inspired leader he had been. If Young Life was to continue to be "the marvelous bandwagon" it had been, there would have to be a new leader.

Seeing Jim crumble was traumatic for everyone—except his own son. Looking back, Jim III realized, "It was after I started seeing Dad's weakness that I began to look on him as a man of God. We started being able to talk to each other. It was a neat thing for me to realize that this guy who was my father was the 'chief among sinners'—like Paul—and yet I could see how much he loved the Lord. As he got more of a human quality and less of a deity quality, he got much easier for me to relate to."

Jim must have sensed the danger he faced. Even in illness, he could not conceive of himself being separated from the position to which he had given virtually all of his life. He called a meeting of his closest friends—Starr, Riviere, Mitchell, and a few others—and demanded that they support him in the face of any action the board might take.

His exhortations were futile. The board, convening in Chicago, had already decided on its course of action.

As tactfully as possible, a committee, headed by directors Stover, Muncy, and Weyerhaeuser, came to inform Jim that they felt he must devote a year to improving his health. They suggested psychiatric treatments as well as rest. If he was himself again at the end of the year, they added, his title and status could be restored. But until then—

In June of 1964, Jim Rayburn was "promoted" to the position of director emeritus, and Bill Starr was asked to take over the management of the mission. A night letter went out right away to all staff, as well as absent board members: "After much prayer and deliberation, the National Board of Directors has unanimously selected Bill Starr as Associate Executive Director and General Manager, effective immediately. The Board asks you to join in prayer for Jim Rayburn's health and for Bill Starr in his new responsibility."

32

WHILE THESE were dark days in many ways, there was resurrection as well as death. The Lord was turning the mission around at the changing of the guard. Three men at headquarters fumbled to help Bill pull the new regime into working order.

John Carter was the only one who carried over from Rayburn's office force. Frayne Gordon came in from managing Malibu, bringing a background of experience as a trouble-shooting manager for a Vancouver forest products company. Bill Taylor, a Chicago committeeman during Starr's term as Midwest regional director, left a career at Argonne National Laboratory. He brought a master's degree in business administration, and a contemporary viewpoint on running a central office with electronic machines and procedures.

These men did for headquarters what Starr and Mitchell had done for the field operation. "The new system and procedures pulled us out of the primitive era," Starr said, "into something that could function on behalf of the staff. What we didn't know was that God was gearing us up for growth."

Although the new team had set out to function in a business-

Headquarters staff, Colorado Springs, 1969. Bill Taylor, extreme right.

like manner, they soon found themselves in the drag of a critical crisis. America's teenagers were spending twenty-five billion dollars a year, much of it on cigarettes, marijuana, alcohol and other drugs, but money was lagging discouragingly at Young Life.

"The last five years of strife and confusion had taken its toll on the mission. Everything came home to roost in the spring of 1967," Taylor said. "We were in technical bankruptcy. Our assets were frozen. We had borrowed some $600,000 from the bank. Our properties were all mortgaged. And we could not meet the April payroll."

Again God's resources were opened up through a rescuing gift from board member C. Davis Weyerhaeuser. Then committees throughout the country set up an emergency Forward Fund Drive, and most of the obligations were met. The curve upward was dramatic. And the mission staggered to its feet.

In the meantime, Bill was quietly calling on the ministers in Colorado Springs to express a philosophy he later recorded in a report to the staff, "When Young Life goes into any area, we realize that the movement of God is already taking place there among His people. God doesn't arrive when we arrive. He's already at work through the church. We are joining in that movement. Local congregations have people and resources which, when combined with ours, can serve to expand God's purposes in remarkable ways."

Gently and without dramatic pronouncements, Bill gained the confidence and fellowship of some of the men he visited.

"In many ways the interim between the visionary who starts something and the ultimate leader of an organization has to be a bridge," board member Stover observed. "In most cases it's an unenviable job, and often covers a very short period of history. Usually the man becomes a sacrificial leader. In changing the pace or the pattern of the entrepreneur, he may have to sacrifice himself. Somehow Bill was able to live around that. He kept the operation moving successfully. He kept the ministry intact . . . and it must have taken a lot of spiritual depth and control that most of us will never know about. I'm sure Bill must have paid some high prices for that."

Bill Starr

33

STARR HAD BEEN shaped in a day when authority characterized leadership. In World War II he was a sailor who took orders, and an officer who gave them; but listening to kids at the ranch and in his clubs also molded him. When he stepped into his new role, he was a man who believed in the servant leader: he was not at the front pulling or in the rear pushing; he was mixed into the whole, learning and following as well as commanding.

No longer was America a land of the hero. Its citizens were entering an era of the debunker, an era of vast suspicion.

In a day when the young were in revolt against established order of any kind, it became extraordinarily appropriate to personalize truth in human beings who could be known and respected. God brought Bill into the executive position at a time when his gentle concern for people's lives, and his funny, quiet joy in the Master of men, made his leadership believable.

As Bill looked over his heritage in the mission, two distinctives emerged clearly: "One, we are a leader-oriented crowd; and two, we believe that the heart of truth is embodied in Jesus Christ."

By leader-oriented he meant that they start with the selection and training of an adult, instead of primarily training kids to reach kids. It meant that the adult was trained to build a per-

108

Young Life Denver committeemen. Left to right: Don Reeverts, Bob Strawn, Chuck Cooke, Howard Parker, Al Swanson

sonal bridge so he or she could cross into the land of the young. This followed the same pattern God used when Christ personally entered planet Earth—to flesh out His plan for the world in ordinary, everyday encounters.

"Truth found in the person of Christ" is the primary statement the mission sought to make—through every endeavor, no matter how simple or how costly. "We have come to believe that truth is bigger than any creed or doctrine," Bill said, "that at best, any of us can only learn an infinitesimal amount of truth in a lifetime . . . that only as we combine the truth we perceive with the truths others see, that we increase our understanding of who God is and who we are . . . and that meeting the Son of God is central to all the rest of living."

By now it was apparent that rather than being a youth movement, Young Life was really a network of grownups who cared about life in all its expressions. Adults who gravitated to Young Life seemed to be those who lived out the freedom and joy and love that should accompany a spiritual breakthrough, but was so often missing in those who called themselves Christian. It was an attractive community, and people wanted to be part of it. Here was light. Here was adventure, enthusiasm, fun, and personal concern. And to the outsider it all seemed deeply rooted in the Creator God who had molded the mountains and flung the stars. Yet somehow it was also a kind of holy hilarity vibrating from these people. Their lifestyle showed a *joie de vivre* that people rarely display without a cocktail, and their hope, even in the midst of disturbance, was enviable.

While displaying a truth is not necessarily teaching it, Bill sensed that he needed a means of communication that could perhaps multiply the effect one person's life could have on another. People had always said there was no way the personal touch could be duplicated and packaged for a larger market, but Bill was about to try. He was eager to go on record in print with some of the good things God had been teaching the staff—through his Word, and through kids.

It was a committee friend of Bill's in Chicago who suggested that they publish a journal for adults instead of reviving the magazine for teenagers. Tom Morris had three popular teenage daughters who provided him a firsthand acquaintance with the "generation gap" of the '60s. He also knew the strengthening effect of Bill's faith and friendship on his own quite new love for the Savior. Here again the Spirit of God moved—this time to bring Morris's professional background in public relations and sales promotion at precisely the right time to actualize Starr's vision for a means of communicating.

They asked a mutual friend to join them for a planning conference in Colorado Springs. Some twenty years earlier, on the campus of Wheaton College, Charlotte Meredith had responded warmly to the Young Life approach and in a journalism class had struck up an intense friendship with staff member Wanda Ann Mercer. Now widowed, and the mother of a Young Life camper-son, Char was determined to put words together to make a living. There seemed no more challenging vehicle in sight than "the marvelous bandwagon."

Out of the conference with the headquarters people came a very thin sixteen-page black-and-white quarterly, which they called *Focus on Youth*. It set out to encourage and to unify, yes; but beyond that it sought to explore, even to probe, what was going on in the rebel culture of the young in the late '60s.

Suddenly half of the American population was under twenty-five, and the teenager was the prize plum of the commercial marketplace. Here was the most beautiful, most widely traveled, healthiest, wealthiest, best-educated adolescent in the world's history. He was surveyed and publicized, romanced and exploited until, frankly, he was fed up and disillusioned with the production-crazed world that put everything at his fingertips.

The revolt that ensued on high school and college campuses was quelled in one place only to burst out in another. Much of what provoked this generation appeared to stem from the shallowness they felt in the family and in society. What they individually selected to fill the nagging void was usually a temporary stopgap pleasure, which occasionally expanded in a pathetic and irreversible harm.

By the time the Young Revolution had left its mark—not all of it bad—the statement of affirmations which appeared in the first issue of *Focus* seemed almost too simple.

Planning each issue of *Focus* over the next eight years required an unexpected output of mental and spiritual energy on the part of the administrative core group at headquarters. For in the process of taking on a journalistic venture, they also found that they were wrestling with the very substance of the new Young Life. Probing the roots of the nationwide youth demonstration while still holding onto their Christian hope tested each of them. What the words and graphics in each finished issue said to the diverse audience of parents and staff could only marginally express what the assignment was teaching the men and women who pooled their resources to bring it about.

During the summer after Martin Luther King's death, Starr came out with an issue of *Focus* to declare openly that the city was as viable and integral a part of Young Life as the suburbs. Its cover carried the photo of a strong young black, with the caption, "I'm not a problem. I'm a man." And its pages were

Chesney and
Chicago friends

opened to black writers and photographers to reveal their beauty
and strengths as well as their anger and hurt.

It was a deep conviction of Starr's that he had to state publicly: prejudice is wrong. "That issue was a milestone in our
history, an act of obedience that stimulated growth," he explained. "We did suffer; but we grew out of that experience.
Until we came out and made the statement visible—and took
whatever suffering that obedient act required—we could not
grow beyond that point."

A few longtime friends questioned, or even withdrew, their
support because of this forthright stand, but there were new
people who rallied around the radical commitment to the op-
pressed which this *Focus* confirmed.

From the urban work going on in Chicago, George Sheffer
discovered a disturbing lack. "On the South Side, where we
were pretty much a social action agency, we found no leadership growing up among our kids. On the West Side, where Jim
Chesney and I combined a proclamation of the Gospel with
our social action, kid after kid moved on into college or other
training. We threatened, coaxed, promised—did everything we
could think of to help them get through high school. There
were twenty who graduated from college out of that early West

112

Side group—some of them beautiful Christians, serving their own people in a number of significant ways."

What was producing lasting results in the streets of the city— or wherever they went—was that powerful combination of the proclamation of Christ, plus the social action that made it real.

34

To WALK FROM the headquarters building to the home of the Rayburns took barely ten minutes, but the gulf that had been created between Jim and the new headquarters team was wide and difficult to cross. An occasional staff member hurried to the little mesa on which the house stood, but others were conspicuous by their absence. It was not easy to see Jim sitting in the big chair brooding. And in the trauma of this debilitating void there was deep ache and loneliness. All that was learned over the years about "relationship" was put to the ultimate test here, and often there was more failure than success—on both sides of the gulf. Many held their confused feelings inside, knowing neither how to explain what was happening, nor how to express their concern.

The Psalms of David ministered to Jim during these days, and he began to see things he had never seen before, but the struggle was intense along the twin trails of his humanity and his spirit. "Our biggest problem as a board," Bob Stover said, "was to get Jim to see that the mission belonged to Jesus Christ, not to him."

Illness plagued both Maxine and Jim—everything from heart failure to convulsions—and it seemed to onlookers that when Jim was strong Maxine was down; and when Jim became ill, Maxine rose. "There's a reason for that," Maxine explained later. "Jim was a very scary person to live with if you really loved him—and I did. When he was strong, I saw him on a disaster course, headed for a breakdown, and he didn't need me. When he was ill, I rallied to take care of his needs."

There were times when Jim couldn't remember anything, and he would ask Maxine the same questions over and over. Miraculously he recovered, and his health stabilized enough in the spring of 1969 so that he suddenly took off for South America. His son, who had graduated from college, accompanied him. Jim had always traveled first class, but when he went abroad he would stay in a mud hut if he thought it would help him get along with the people.

"We'd sit in the sun in some foreign place," his son reported, "or meet some college kids in a restaurant or climb on some rickety old bus. Dad was in his world. He was in paradise. And I'd be thinking, 'Lord, what are we doin' out here in the boondocks of Argentina?' At the end of a 24-hour day, he'd kinda look at me and say, 'Pretty tough day, huh? But look at all the contacts we made. Boy! I wish I could stay down here. I wish I had more time.' I could see how Young Life got built against incredible odds. He would never say die!

"I never saw such compassion. We'd come back to the hotel after being out all day, sometimes bad-mouthed up one side and down the other by a mob of kids who were not only closed to Americans, but especially to *Christian* Americans. But Dad would say, 'Jim, what chance are these people gonna have to know Christ if we're not gonna tell 'em?' And he'd look at me and say, 'Don't ever think you can leave it up to someone else.' He was hoping I'd get the vision, and I did," said young Rayburn.

Out of this trip, Jim started an entirely new mission called Youth Research International to pioneer Young Life methods in other countries. On his return to the states, he asked Bill Taylor to be chairman of the board, and Jim III went over to Brazil to work with the new organization. There he married Lucia, a petite and vibrant Brazilian girl, and they were quite prepared to spend the rest of their lives in South America.

114

Shortly after their marriage, a letter arrived from home: "Don't worry about it. Don't change your plans. Just thought I ought to let you know I've got cancer. Love, Dad."

"Dad put me in a tough spot," Jim said later. "It was the same old lack of family emphasis, like, 'I'm dying, Jim, but stay there and do the Lord's work. Don't sweat me.' My reaction was, 'I'll get down here later if need be, but you're dying, Dad, and home's where I'm going to be!' I think he was very glad that we came. He thought Lucia hung the moon, and when our little Shannon was born, he was thrilled to have a granddaughter."

Jim's attitude toward death was phenomenal. He was very matter-of-fact about leaving this world, and there were things he wanted to accomplish and people he wanted to see. On several occasions he would go over to Trail West Lodge to stay, but first he called the manager, John Miller, to make sure the old friends there wouldn't treat him as if he were in a zoo. He didn't want people looking at him to see how a dying person acts. "We know what's going on," he said. "So treat me normal."

One night John Miller heard a knock on his bedroom door. It was 3:45 A.M. He opened the door and saw Jim leaning against the corridor wall, "Don't you want some ice cream, John?" Without any hesitation, John fired back, "Yeah, Jim. I've just been layin' here wishin' somebody would invite me out." Over the big bowls of ice cream, Jim confided, "I can't get used to the fact that God's gonna take me home soon, cuz I'm sure he's got a lot of things he wants me to do. And I'm afraid he's gonna let some 'inferior' guy do 'em for me." Then he looked at John with a little grin, and no more was said.

Later one of the work crew girls who was serving Jim's table in the dining room asked him, "Would you take a message to my mother? She's been gone a couple years, and we didn't get along very well. I wonder if you'd tell her I love her?" Jim put his arm around her and said, "I'll be glad to, honey, but I'll be late. She knows that."

At home he would sit on the landing above the living room near his bookshelves. There were days when nobody would

115

come to see him or send him a card, and he'd say, "Where are my people?"

"I think the ones he longed to have near him stayed away because they didn't know what to say," Maxine reflected. "That's why I stayed so close. I hardly let him out of my sight. I realized so much of what had happened was because I had failed him. The victory for us came in the final days and months of excruciating pain when Jim had time to express his love to me. This is what I remember so well."

Weekends Jim would call his old friend. "Hey, Benson, the game's started. Aren't you comin' over?" Never much of a football fan himself, Ted was on call all fall. Jim's favorite team was Oklahoma, and he had gone out of his way several times to talk with Wilkinson, whom he considered football king of the world.

Watching the TV screen, he would turn to Ted and say, "Those fellas don't know it, but they're God's agents to me in my predicament to help me through these days."

"Jim wasn't going to be one of those people who would lie in bed and let people wait on him," Benson described. "He'd get up and actually struggle to hang onto the door, then step over and grab hold of the top of the chair, and let himself down into the seat. He did that till he lost consciousness and went into a coma."

The week before that happened, Jim sensed the time was closing in on him. Two Argentina friends, visiting the Rayburns, drove him downtown one day. He went to his barber to get a shampoo and a massage. He went to see the banker who had handled his financial matters. He went to his travel agent and bought a ticket to Los Angeles. And he stopped in at Headquarters to see his Young Life friends. This was at a time when he could barely sit on a chair more than half an hour because his spinal discs were deteriorating.

Early Saturday morning, Jim's nurse drove him over to Jim and Lucia's home. He got out of the car in his robe and slippers. He wanted to see his little granddaughter. "I could kick myself," Jim III said later, "because I was asleep. He came in and sat

116

on my bed for ten minutes or so, and never woke me up—apparently just watched me sleep."

Later that afternoon the young Rayburns stopped by the house on the mesa to see Jim. He was curled on the bed in terrible pain. The last thing his son ever said to him was about the airline reservation to L.A. In love, he bawled him out, "You just quit tryin' to fly outa here, Dad, and let us take care of you!"

At three o'clock the next morning, Jim got a phone call saying his dad had slipped. He immediately went back over to be with his parents. Later in the day a pastor friend who had known Jim since the Dallas days stopped by. Everyone thought Jim was unconscious as Harlan Harris opened the Bible and read from the Scripture; but Jim whispered, "I know that one." He never spoke after that. On December 11, 1970, with Mitch and Bill Taylor and the family gathered around the bed, Jim moved on out beyond the reach of further pain and frustration. They were reading the Twenty-third Psalm. A wild canary sang in the evergreen. And Mitch wept silently by the window. "He considered Mitch his son," Jim III mentioned. "He loved him as much as he did me."

Since Jim had willed his body to the University of Colorado Medical School for research, Bill Taylor called Denver to let them know Jim had died. Later in the day an old gray Ford wagon rattled up La Mesa Road and into the driveway. Two young med students in lab coats knocked at the door. A few minutes later they carried Jim's body out on a stretcher, loaded it into the station wagon, and disappeared down the road in a cloud of dust. Jim himself couldn't have planned the details more fittingly. He had slipped the bonds of the painful old clay shell and could very well be laughing hilariously as the car sped north on the Denver freeway.

"In spite of the massive amount of problems he had, Dad would think of a joke and he'd giggle like a ten-year-old," Jim III said. "When I think of him, I think of funny things. He was funny to the very end."

117

35

TWENTY YEARS after Jerry Kirk prayed with his buddy on the big rock near Frontier, he brought fifteen families with him to Trail West Lodge. Mark and Doris Trabert came along from Jerry's church in Cincinnati. Mark was a lawyer—the kind of man who could be so honest with Jerry about where he was with God. Several times Jerry was invited to speak somewhere, and he would ask Mark to go along and share. Mark would say, "Well, Jerry, you know I'm not committed." And Jerry usually answered, "That's OK. I want you to tell your story. I know a lot of church people who aren't as committed as you." Mark had an effect on people just through his openness.

At Trail West the Traberts accompanied John Miller to Frontier Ranch where they all sat on the floor with the kids during the Round Up meeting. The leader spoke vividly about the crucifixion of Christ. Then he gave everyone twenty minutes to go out of the Kachina Lodge in silence to think through what they had heard. Jerry walked down the hill to the familiar old rock, where a kid was already sitting. In the light of a billion Colorado stars, he recognized his own son. Jerry sat down beside him and waited. As they started back up the hill together, Mark and Doris came by, arm in arm. Recognizing the two ahead of them on the path, Mark put his arms around Jerry and embraced him vigorously. "I'm committed, Jerry!" he exclaimed. "I just gave my life to Christ to do whatever He wants to do with it."

Less than half a year later, Mark Trabert died in a plane crash. John Miller left Trail West to represent Young Life at the funeral, but he made the trip knowing he had lost a new friend. In the church he was handed a program printed with the words, "Welcome to the celebration of the resurrection of Mark Trabert."

During the service, Jerry opened his pulpit to anyone who wanted to give a witness for the Lord, or pay tribute to Mark.

In the audience were family, friends, colleagues, neighbors, civic leaders, corporate executives. His old Young Life friend, Marv Heaps, now president of ARA Food Services, stepped out and said, "Mark had but one wish—that was for his family, his relatives and friends to know Jesus Christ as he did."

Five other people stood, one a client of Mark's. Unsure, deeply moved, she spoke haltingly, "Mark Trabert meant everything to me. He changed my whole life. I never felt as close to anyone as I did to him." She went on to explain that she had wondered why they could feel so close, and Mark had told her, "Maybe it's because we've been through so much garbage together." Later John Miller found out that she was part of the swinger set, and had gone to Trabert's office for legal counsel on a divorce. Through Mark's influence she had crossed over into a new life with Christ—and with her husband.

A man, who had been awaiting Mark's arrival in Florida when the plane crashed, walked up to the pulpit and said, "Jerry, would you mind just standing here by me? Because I'm not committed yet."

"It was the first funeral I'd ever been to," John said, "where tears and laughter were so beautifully mixed."

Rayburn had dreamed of Trail West as a showplace where

Trail West; Emile Cailliet with Rayburn

he could bring people who could "invest" in Young Life. He wanted a kind of "window" through which family and friends could view what went on at Frontier Ranch and Silver Cliff. He had hiked through the aspen grove on the old horse ranch many times. It was a small piece of heaven that he wanted to share. As he was sitting on a lichen-spattered boulder in the middle of the rocky hillside, God said, "Build it here." Spread out before him, in the sublime presence of Mt. Princeton, lay a wide valley, set with tiny Buena Vista's huddle of shops and homes. Just by being in that beautiful place Jim expected the world would be curious. People would come and ask, What is it, and what is happening here, and what is the real angle behind it? The only thing that surprised him was that it took so long for the world to start catching on to Trail West, knocking on its door, asking the reason for the hope that is inside.

What God had in mind turned out to be an even broader use of Jim's concept: not just a place for wealthy donors, but a family resort where everyone could come—a church, a neighborhood, a Young Life committee, a therapy group—to pursue whatever nudging they felt from God. People arrive as guests, and leave as friends. So much of the essence of Trail West lies in the people who make it happen—the Body of Christ quietly serving in so many little ways. The work crew is the number one influence. John Miller is constantly asked, "What makes these young people different?" And John says, "Well, I don't know your kids, but I know what makes these kids tick. They know Jesus Christ, and there's nothing in the world they'd rather do than serve Him. They pay their own way out to Colorado. They pay their own way home. They put in eight hours a day of hard work and don't get paid a cent. Then they go home and write glowing letters of thanks for the privilege of growing in Christ for one month together." John chuckles and adds, "That's the only difference I know."

One evening Bill Starr sat on the balcony at the Lodge with a new friend, a man from the Lilly Foundation in Indianapolis. Looking out over the wooded slopes beyond the aspens, and upward to the granite peak, he shared with Charles Williams the miracles God had wrought, and the rapid growth that was

Above: Trail
West Lodge.
Right: John
Miller and Mt.
Princeton

stretching every ounce of resource that he could muster. Williams had just returned from the Round Up at Frontier, enthused about the first-class music, the expert entertainment, and the simple compelling presentation of the gospel. Returning the next day to his Indianapolis office, Williams continued the relationship with Starr. Out of that encounter at Trail West God opened up a series of grants from Lilly which culminated in a million dollars designated for training of Young Life leadership. It was one of the largest grants ever made by the foundation in its "religious" category.

36

COMING OF AGE during the '60s raised the consciousness level of the mission—toward training, toward family, toward camping, toward the church. "We were moving from being this funny little thing attached like an appendix on the perimeter of the organized church to centering ourselves within that body and existing for the benefit of that body," Bob Reeverts said. "To come to grips with who we are in relation to the whole Christian family is going to be a point of real maturity."

Ever since the Chicago Fellowship gathering in 1960, the Spirit of God was saying, "Don't try to keep it. Give it away with no strings attached." One man who left that Fellowship meeting carried the seed of vitality back to the Twin Cities, to Luther Seminary, where he was president with a new vision. Al Rogness invited Rayburn and Shoemaker to speak to his student body. The result was both immediate and lasting. The standing ovation —the only such response Rogness can recall—seemed to be not so much for the men who spoke, but for the Christ who was so vivid in their lives. Out of one man's readiness, God began to pull together the Minnesota Youth Leadership with two of the Young Life staff in the area, Phil McDonald and Ken Wright.

122

Later five denominational seminaries crossed all boundaries to come together in a training program that combines theological study and practical work for Young Life staff and other youth ministers. Jim had started by taking his earliest staff members through a consistent study of the gospels, using Dr. Chafer's *Systematic Theology.* He loved to learn, and he loved to teach. He wanted to build excellence into the staff. He wanted them to be educated—to know what they were talking about. "He was persuaded that we needed the best, most up-to-date instruction we could get," remembered Dick Langford. "He led us in a way that made us open to learn new things."

By the late '40s when Tom Raley wanted to leave staff to go to seminary, Jim complained that seminary training had a negative effect on his leaders—it diminished their love of the Savior and cut into his ranks. While most of them enrolled anyway, they knew that a faster way to train leadership was brewing in his mind.

Over the years Jim had met and respected men such as Emile Cailliet, Donald Gray Barnhouse, Frank Gaebelein, Lawrence Kulp; and he wanted his staff to learn from them too. With the help of Dr. Kulp and Wally Howard, the Young Life Institute opened in the summer of 1954. It was an adventure in excellence which has affected thousands of leader-learners—both Young Life career and volunteer staff, plus representatives from many churches and parachurch ministries. In the seclusion of the Spanish cloisters and spacious campus of the Fountain Valley School for Boys, outstanding professors from many graduate schools share their expertise in biblical and practical studies during two summer terms.

The training of leadership, which started on a one-to-one, hand-holding kind of basis, has gone through several significant stages. The Young Life Fellowship on college campuses expanded into a Leadership Training Week held regionally and annually at the different campsites. Always men like Benson, Howard, Starr, and Mitchell agreed with Rayburn's belief that education of leaders must never stop. It cannot be static, but must continuously enrich itself with the stimulation of new knowledge, new discovery.

Leadership Seminar at Trail West

Training becomes more imperative as more people get involved. Over the years, Bob Mitchell grew naturally to the place where it was appropriate for him to be named vice-president of training in 1975. From his earliest response to Rayburn in the Campaign tent in Dallas until the present day, he has been immersed in every aspect of Young Life. "It's easy to get some soft things going here and there that don't look like us," Mitch said. "Maybe it's a theological degeneration, or a club ministry that isn't reaching out, or a lack where the strategies for reaching into the community are not thought out. Any of these can cause a funny-looking little aardvark thing to happen—just because somebody wasn't trained."

Three tracks are laid for training. One is the normal seminary education. The second requires a college education, plus enrollment at the Young Life Institute for four summers. That combination earns a Master of Arts degree. In addition, the person is assigned during the winter to a specific area for on-the-job experience and participation in a Regional Training Program. The third is the Masters' Program. This is a theological curriculum, supplemented by field work on a one-to-one basis with a Young Life training director. It leads to a Master of Arts in Youth Ministry degree.

Again God used Dr. Rogness, this time in dialogue with Ken Wright and Starr from Young Life, and Dr. David Hubbard,

124

Staff members in training

president of Fuller Seminary in Pasadena. Starting at Luther with Dick Lowey as director, the Masters' Program branched out to Fuller with Jim Shelton; North Park with Bud Ipema in Chicago; and Gordon-Conwell with Dean Borgman in Boston.

Young Life trainers meet on a regular schedule to share ideas and increase their skills to meet more effectively the needs of the field. They are searching for ways to give trainees more definitive help for the complex job of area director. "When I started out," Shelton remembered, "my field was ridiculous— eighty miles—from south San Francisco to Gilroy. I saw my area director once a month. I don't know how I survived. I don't know how he did either." Twenty years later demands are more complex.

"I'm moving toward more supervision, a little tighter ship— asking harder questions, making each seminarian more responsible, stretching more," says Borgman. "We live very close to each other during these seminary years. They're in one of my classes all the way through the program. They get supervision both from the field staff and from me. Plus they have a weekly group situation with each other—just the M.A. students."

"What we're doing," Mitch explained, "is providing teaching within the structure of the church. The classes are open to any seminarian. It's a chance to give ourselves away at the same time that we prepare our staff more adequately. The seminaries allow the training director to develop his own curriculum."

At Gordon-Conwell, Borgman uses a research project out on

the streets of Boston to start students relating to the real needs of men and women. They interview the town clerk, chief of police, garbage collector, a waitress, a gas station attendant, high school custodian, kids in the park—and they come back truly excited.

"They haven't had to witness to them," Borgman said, "they've just been able to talk with them. They learn to listen to what it is that people are concerned about. It's become a very stimulating device in learning to communicate the gospel."

Borgman accompanied one of his trainees to a new town where no Young Life person had visited. It was one of three towns served by a regional high school. It had two churches— one Protestant, one Catholic. "We stopped first to see the town clerk," said Borgman, "and he sent us around to the Methodist minister. The priest and the minister had set up a teenage drop-in center on Friday nights. The minister was glad to have someone he could talk to about what was going on. He mentioned having a $1400 item in his budget for a seminarian to help out with the youth work. I picked up on that, and later was able to follow through to the advantage of all of us. As a result, the trainee, who was a slow starter at the seminary, has blossomed in that position with the church. He's married and moved into a little apartment in that town. The minister and the priest are thrilled to have a man who knows how to work with their kids . . . and we have an added $1400 in our budget for training!"

In Chicago at North Park Seminary there are two urban programs. One, newly endowed by Lilly, is directed by Oliver Trimiew, solely to prepare black students for ministry. The other is designed to share urban knowledge and experience with the general Young Life staff. It's a four-week urban sensitivity study term which now supplements the traditional camp assignment for a certain number of staff. "Since there are no longer enough camp spots for all our leaders, some of them now come to Chicago for a month instead of going to camp," Ipema grins. "They live in the ghetto with black or Puerto Rican families, and we study intensively the whole urban scene.

"First, we deal with their own attitudes; then four weeks later we measure the attitudinal change. Then we deal with urban systems—political, economic, educational. Then we visit working models of urban ministry: Pace Institute, LaSalle Street Church, several black churches. Finally, we move into a specific area of problem such as housing. We study that in depth for a week. We tour the metropolitan area, see destruction in old areas of the city, look at public housing, in-between communities, and new outlying subdivisions. Wherever we go we talk with the people. What causes housing problems? Who are the allies, the enemies? How can we correct the problem?

"I'm strong on seeing solutions," Bud explained, "so people can come out of the city with some sense of celebration, some hope. We find the surrounding community really surprised to see the seminary outside of its walls," Bud smiled. "Our main idea is to expose as many of our staff as we can to some urban study, and to get them out into the streets of the neighborhood to dig out their own resources."

In Florida, Charlie Scott says, "It's encouraging here to be getting calls from churches. One asked, 'Can you teach an adult series for six weeks?' Another wants someone who is trained to work with their youth program. A Presbyterian pastor asked if his church could pay part of the salary of one of our staff men. It is beautiful to see them wanting to work with us, and yet wanting us to be ourselves. It makes what we can do in the future so awe-inspiring."

37

THE WOMEN who were drawn to Young Life in the Dallas days were very much a major part of the mission. Jim had known for a long time that they needed women to relate to the high school girls coming to club. And he needed someone to handle secretarial details even before he moved into his tiny seminary office.

Ollie Dustin, a high school girl who helped with the Houston tent Campaign, was the first to arrive. Later, as a full-time secretary to the president of Inter-Coastal Canal Association, she provided an additional service for a man on the move with no budget. She would work frantically for several days at a time while her boss was in the office. Then he would go on the road, and Ollie had nothing to do for weeks except answer the phone. When Jim Rayburn discovered how well Ollie took dictation, he asked her to help with his growing correspondence. "Jim would come into the office and dictate," Ollie recalled. "Then he would fall asleep on the sofa while I transcribed his dictation. I was petrified that my boss might walk in . . . but he never did. Jim was unbelievable." Ollie added, "The relationship was one of mutual admiration and respect. His concepts of how to reach people were so different from my church background. He made the Bible such an everyday part of my life." How much Ollie's boss would have agreed with her is debatable—if he'd known that for two years Young Life had a Houston headquarters with all the facilities Jim needed—at no cost!

After Ollie, came Kay MacDonald and Sarah Bransford from Memphis, Annie Cheairs from Little Rock, and Wanda Ann Mercer from Winnfield, Louisiana. All of them came out of an almost manless church society. To find men who were excited about the Scripture and who talked about it naturally, with clarity, and in depth, surprised and pleased them.

"The thing that first awakened my personal interest in Young Life was the fact that it was run and staffed by men," Kay Mac said. "I came from a small church which was dominated by 'spiritual' women."

"In those days," Wally Howard remembers, "there was a good deal of unresolved tension about our respective roles. A lot of insecurity on the part of the men, not knowing how to relate to the obvious abilities of those women who worked so hard along with us. There was a lot of talk about how effective a woman could be as a club leader." The conclusion at that time was that the woman's role was a supportive one. The man was the leader. The woman would work as his assistant. In the small Bible study groups she could lead the girls' sessions.

From the night Riviere sat on the balcony at Frontier years

later and asked Starr, "What do we do with women?" until the storming of the country by women's lib, it was only a matter of time. The steps were quietly taken but cumulative. Today the official statement has gone out: a woman can fill any position for which she can qualify, and at the same salary as a man in the same position.

In 1971, Grace Preedy, a staff woman who had made significant contributions to the work in Brazil, talked with Bill Taylor at staff conference. She would like to develop her gifts more fully, but she didn't know how much Young Life would hold for her in the future. She wanted to train women in Young Life, and Taylor urged her to put her thoughts in writing. These were sent to Starr and Mitchell at headquarters, and to Bob Reeverts who was then a divisional vice-president in her area around San Francisco.

After the Institute some months later, Mitch announced that the staff manual had been revised so that it read, "The area director shall be a *person*," whereas previously it had explicitly stated, "The area director shall be a *man*."

Someone asked him how he and Starr came to make this change. In answer he told a story. On a recent flight he had talked with the young woman seated next to him. She was twenty-eight years old and a lawyer. In the government agency where she was employed she had a staff of twelve working under her.

When Mitch recovered from that shock, she asked him what he did, and followed up with a question about how women fit into Young Life. "I realized we didn't have a leg to stand on," Mitch admitted, "and that we couldn't wait any longer to begin exploring new ways to use the gifts of our staff women."

That fall, 1972, Grace Preedy was given the go-ahead for a training program for staff girls on the West Coast. In October, Mitch asked Dr. Paul Jewett, director of the Young Life Institute, to come to an area directors' meeting to present a paper, "Man as Male and Female." Jewett insisted that some women must be present for the discussion that would follow. Gail Grimston and Lil Runnion were invited for that one day. They discussed what the Bible has to say regarding women in the church, and the matter of their own personal feelings. Then

129

Mitch told them there were two reasons that made him feel so strongly the need to revise the place of women in Young Life; first, the growing recognition of women in the larger world; and second, the increasing pile of letters from disappointed staff women over the years. He left the impression that something had to change. One of his first acts was to hire Beverly Wear and Julie Anderton to assist him in the Training Department.

Since then all women have the same opportunities for theological training open to them as men do; some married women have been employed as field staff with reasonable success; single men and women are on the same salary scale; and the first women have been invited to serve on the board of directors—a former staff woman, Marge Petersen, and a volunteer leader, Dora Hillman.

Others whose inner demands were so strong they had to go elsewhere before the freedom came still feel as Wanda Ann Mercer did when she told of Add Sewell's encouragement to her, "God is committed to lead you. He has no choice. He said He would. There's not a prayer that He won't." And WAM's comment from the university campus at which she now teaches was, "That's the sort of encouragement we had in Young Life constantly between people. Just bedrock simplicity that will work wherever you are on this earth."

From the days of cleaning three little cubbyholes in Dallas, emptying wastebaskets, mopping the floor, and handling the details you were told to do, you have come a long way, baby!

38

GOING INTO the city had made George Sheffer very conscious of the aberrations of society. Kids who broke out of the everyday structures of home and school needed to be loved and heard and attended to in a special way. Not just the inner-city ghetto kids, but middle-class white youngsters piled up personal vendettas and looked for relief in some form of socially unacceptable behavior. What was emerging was the fact that the difference between the young person in the city and the one in the suburbs was not as great as the sociologists had thought. The adolescent community has many characteristics in common, regardless of where it hangs its hat.

"This is what made Young Life useful," Starr said. "We were finding out that anything we learned in one portion of society overlapped and became a useful tool in other aspects of society."

In the '70s, America had moved full speed into the chemical age. The marijuana issue was hot. Narcotics were taking over the suburbs; some of what kids learned to count on for their mood changes came out of the family medicine chest. The runaway rate was on the rise as nice kids from nice homes pocketed Daddy's credit cards and took off. By the time they got to Colorado, they were often tired, hungry, sick, or out of money. The Springs seemed as good a place as any to build a halfway house.

It was 1971 when Starr, Mitchell, and Taylor called Shef to see if he would start a program to train leaders to work with the alienated kids who were running rampant over the highways and the parks of the world. *"Would* I?" Sheffer responded. That very thing had been his dream for many months. Here, perhaps more than in any other aspect of Young Life, the wisdom of "a life on a life" was essential.

By January, 1972, after reviewing and interviewing young people from all over the United States, he had drawn together a team. These were the backbone of the project called Dale House, named after the street where the crash house was located. Team members weren't far beyond adolescence themselves, and most of them knew what it felt like to be high—and to crash.

Shef knew he could handle the biblical training of the team, but he needed help in other areas. His own son, George III, who had just returned from Viet Nam, stepped in to organize the practical aspects of the program.

Jim Oraker and his wife, Judy, had been praying several years

Dale House: Jim
Oraker, left;
George Sheffer,
right.

about a place in the Young Life family. With the opening of
Dale House in Colorado Springs, they recognized their call and
joined the staff shortly after the team started to gather. Dr.
Oraker had come up through Young Life club, campaigners,
and work crew. At Fuller Seminary he received the highest
award in his graduating class for the integration of theology and
psychology, and then was licensed by the State of California
as a practicing psychologist. In a cluster of rambling old houses
this newest pioneer in the organization began working out some
of his beliefs about "family," about community.

Federal figures stated that a million teenagers were running
away each year. Dale House offered a place to run to.

It is a model of hope for a lot of Sues, Toms, Joes, and Marys
who can't make it at home—a loving, caring family that knows
how to coax them into clarifying some goals, and making a run
for a little bit of progress that can be measured. When one of
these kids arrives at even the smallest of goals, self-respect and
joy in achieving start to seep in. The "contract" setup at the
Dale House is not soft; it's tender, but it's tough.

A kid on drugs may be willing to flush his supply down the
toilet when he arrives. If he refuses, he probably will be invited
outside. But . . . it's more than likely that one of the team will
be sitting out on the front steps with him—all night if necessary—until he begins to get the faintest notion that the tough
things they're asking of him are all designed to help him get

132

himself together. The staff accepts a twenty-four-hour responsibility—seeking that balance between being a parent who can hold and comfort and encourage, and being a firm sort of "coach" laying out disciplines to help untangle the knots that make some lives a rat's nest. Three hundred come to the project each year.

"As kids leave home," says Dr. Oraker, "they really aren't rejecting the idea of family; it's just that in most cases they've never experienced a healthy family that knows how to work on caring about each other. That's what we try to provide."

While many kids were running away from home, many more figured they could just cut loose from some of the machines and gadgets they had depended on all their lives and maybe get the same effect. Levis and jeans became almost a uniform. Bicycling came back in with a rush, and hiking boots—or something of that nature—got to be a prized possession. John Denver lured them away from the boob tube, singing, "Sunshine round my shoulders makes me happy," and a whole bunch of America's young decided to check it out.

Stress camping arrived on the Young Life scene just in time. Down at Windy Gap, a new thing called Pioneer Plunge invited

the kids out of the beautifully constructed buildings that had been designed a few years earlier just for them. While the majority elected to stay in the traditional program, there were others who were overjoyed to get off the beaten track. Under experienced guides they shoved miles into the Smokies—built their own shelters, ground their own flour, baked bread, cut timber, drove mules, killed and cleaned small game and cooked it for supper, built rough furniture. And got lonesome, hungry and tired.

Colorado was a natural location for wilderness camping. That's where everybody was heading anyway. The Rockies were a challenge to kids looking for a rugged physical and mental experience. "Putting a fifty-pound pack on your back teaches you pretty fast how to carry your own load," Starr laughed, remembering his own experience at Malibu. "You learn to help each other. And in the process of getting up a difficult place you realize that life is also difficult, and you can't make it on your own any more than you can out here on the cold barren face of that peak."

Kelly, a girl headed for Wilderness Ranch, confessed, "The first day I thought, 'What am I paying all this money for?' I was feeling such anxiety because it hurt just to walk. And I felt a lot of resentment toward Chuck, who was leading." Chuck was an experienced guide—strong, serious, responsible and kind—but Kelly thought, "He can do all that stuff, but here are all of us little weirdos that can't walk like he can. And I thought, 'Golly! Why doesn't he stop?' Those switchbacks were terrors. I tried to be by myself because I was in such a bad mood, and I didn't want to share those feelings with anybody."

By the time the camp began to come to an end everything had changed. "Everybody got so open," Kelly reported. "I'd say right out, 'Boy! I'm really hurting.' The day we were rappelling I'd fall up against the wall and scratch my head on the rock, but it would never totally kill me. And that's the way it is with the Lord. Things bug me every day, and things bring me down, but nothing is ever gonna totally mess me up." Kelly summarized her week, "Confidence would have to be the key word for me—in the Lord and in myself. Confidence was going to get

me down that mountain. Confidence that the Lord was taking care of me. Confidence that I'm as much God's person as anyone else."

Not everybody learns the same thing. While confidence was Kelly's lesson, others learn dependence on others—not trying to do the whole thing alone.

39

AT THE SAME time the kids were leaning on each other in the stress camping programs, Bill Starr was grasping some of the same truth at headquarters. "It was a great learning experience about how life is intertwined with a lot of other people. It has to be a joint effort. You can't make it on your own."

Years earlier John Miller had said, "Just at the time Jim Rayburn had created a mission so large he couldn't handle it, God sent Bill Starr in to be a delegator." And that was what was happening in the '70s. Bill, who by this time had been officially designated as president of Young Life, was tying a lot of strings together. From a one-man mission it had become a team that was learning to function in harmony.

The city was operating under the leadership of Dr. John Porter, a well-prepared vice-president of urban affairs who had gone through the civil rights years with his friend Martin Luther King. Larry Entwistle, who had gotten Woodleaf really humming, became a vice-president in charge of properties. Bob Mitchell had taken over training, as vice-president in that area. Bill Taylor, who had whipped the office into organizational sleekness a decade earlier, was now a vice-president in charge of finance. The team was complete except for the area of administration/communications.

For years Tom Morris, the public relations consultant from Chicago, had flown in and out of the Springs. His generous spirit and warm, good humor made him a welcome addition to the team on a part-time basis. He had been wined and dined and coaxed and begged to consider a move to Colorado, but neither the offer nor the call of God were ever clear enough to uproot him from the Midwest. On a lake in upper Wisconsin, he and Starr had hatched the most recent communications device in a fishing boat. It was a tiny magazine that could be handed out personally to kids at club, gratis. It would carry no advertising. It could be slipped into the pocket of a pair of jeans. It was to be an extension of a club meeting in print, to capture and solidify some of the fleeting new truth a kid picked up at club—something to hold those thoughts till he got home where he could consider them in privacy. With the demise of *Focus on Youth,* the planning team was open to a new vehicle that would carry the gospel in a Young Life style. In the winter of 1975 Tom went home to put together a pilot issue of *Young Life Magazine.* Mitch approved and carried it with him to staff conferences all over the country.

Then out of the blue there was a phone call from Senator Mark Hatfield in the Capitol building. Starr was not surprised to hear from Mark. The senator had served on the Young Life board for quite a few years, and had given wise counsel many times during the "hawk versus dove" days of the Viet Nam war. This time he was calling on a personal conviction. His friend and colleague in Washington, Jeb Stuart Magruder, had served his prison sentence for involvement in Watergate and was looking for a place where he could work on behalf of people. He was through with the "rat race" of the big corporation and wanted to put his knowledge and expertise into something Christian. He and his wife had a personal commitment to the Savior that was tested regularly and was producing new strength and courage daily. Would there be a place in the Young Life team where he would fit?

"My first response was one of shock," Starr recalled. "I was unaware of Jeb, his interests, and how God was leading him. I had no idea he would be interested in a Christian organization until that phone call came. I knew Mark well enough to know he was serious, so I was serious too. I asked John Carter to go with me to meet Jeb at the Denver airport. I wanted to test John's reactions against mine, and we agreed to ask Jeb if he would drive back to Colorado Springs with us, meet the rest of the team, and see the operation at headquarters." Jeb liked what he saw well enough to come back later with his wife, Gail.

"We were in the habit of discouraging people outside the organization from coming into the staff," Starr explained. "It was really tough to make it. The Frayne Gordons, the Bill Taylors were few and far between. We all knew that it would be a difficult thing for someone to come in and fill a top spot right off. But Jeb, Gail and I had a good talk, and they decided they wanted to come. The waiting period before the board took action was really hard on Jeb. But in May 1975 they unanimously approved asking Magruder to come to Young Life as vice-president of administration and communication."

That summer Starr, Taylor, Magruder and others decided to try stress camping themselves. After jogging around Cheyenne Mountain with fifty pounds of *National Geographics* in his back pack, Taylor was ready to leave the accounting department and get acquainted with this new team member from the big time. In the wilds beyond Malibu it didn't take long for any of the men to sense how much they needed each other. "Magruder's first experience with us was on the mountainside," Starr chuckled. "He demonstrated that he was a competitor—not fighting against *us,* but struggling with his own self to refine and increase his personal capacities. And he pushed himself right up that mountain. It was fascinating, and we had a great experience, being exposed to some very difficult tests."

The trip they took was a part of Malibu's "Beyond" program, an idea that started with some of the Canadian staff who thought of a way to give people a view of what the British Columbia country was like, but in a way that would bring them face to face with its ruggedness.

"Out of Malibu," Starr described, "we went up one of the waterways of the Jarvis Inlet. Then we started our ascent into the mountains and gained elevation rapidly. Suddenly we found ourselves walking around on top of the world. This was our experience for five days—the thrill of a glacier with its vast

138

expanse of snow . . . a storm in the middle of summer that literally stopped us in our tracks because we were so blinded by whiteness there wasn't a chance of seeing where we were going . . . the 3,000 foot drops off the mountain. There were four or five of us to a tent, doing everything together. We had to stay together just to survive. By the time we returned to Malibu, we had every chance to know what Jeb was like, and he'd found out what the rest of us were made of too." And it was OK with God and men.

40

IT'S LIKE A chain—" one fellow says, "everybody holding hands around the world." It's God breaking through a million faces. A touch that transcends time and space. It's love flowing from Chafer to Rayburn to Sheffer to Nelson to Reeverts to a million kids.

It's John and Chris Patak with hearts big enough to encompass forty-three "problem kids." It's the city fathers in Rockford blocking off the main street so a bunch of crazy kids can race *beds!* It's Dr. Andy swallowing a live goldfish because the club broke two hundred fifty in attendance and he'd bet they couldn't make it. It's a dozen businessmen in a private club high above Denver talking about ballooning and deep-sea diving and the incredible journey they're on with the Holy Spirit. It's a living room full of mothers listening to a beautiful widow tell them that God loves them as much as he loves their kids.

It's Bob and Mike and Tim and Ed—swimming, riding, racing with Ric Jones till the obscenities of his twisted life were chiseled into a scholarship to attend Cambridge University. It's a bachelor (and former Olympic diver) in Bermuda sitting in his well-worn living room reading the Gospel of Mark with a cluster of young friends, black and white. It's a "circus with a purpose" in Greenville with one hundred seventy people pledging sixteen thousand dollars. It's a surgeon, a psychiatrist, a lawyer, a Vassar-graduate-turned-grandmother, an independent oil producer, and a nucleus of corporation presidents locked into board sessions because they're enthralled with giving kids a chance to meet Christ.

It's ninety guests checking into Trail West Lodge for a "Ski and Grow" week . . . a team of basketball players flying home from Australia where they found God alive on the other side of the globe . . . Dick and Ellen jogging to get in shape for a bicycle trip through the Blue Ridge Mountains . . . Rod and Fran Johnston skiing in the French Alps with a carload of Parisian students . . . Gary and Kathy grubbing in the soil of Israel with fifteen high school students who want to go all the way back to the place where the chain began.

It's Mal McSwain in Atlanta, Carl Nelson in Memphis, Don Taylor in LA, Jerry Johnson in Baltimore, Doug Burleigh in Seattle. It's Bill and Ruth Starr staying in a German convent overwhelmed by the grace of God in the Sisters of Mary. It's Darrell Guder translating words of life for Helmut Thielicke in Berlin and Colorado Springs. It's Don McClean resigning from his position as a high school principal in Menlo Park to spend a year counseling with Young Life. It's Magruder on the platform of a hundred banquets sharing the justice and mercy of God in his family. It's love. It's life. It's God.

It's Jabo Cox at midnight listening to suburban Sandra crying happily into the telephone, "It works! Jabo, it works!" Some weeks earlier Sandra had come up after club and challenged Jabo's statement that the love of Christ can change people.

"You puttin' me on, Jabo, or does it work?" she asked. And he put his arms around her and smiled, "It works, honey."

Sandra was a cheerleader who

141

"It works!"

traveled with the in-crowd. She flipped her shiny hair over her shoulder, looked Jabo in the eye, and said, "We'll see."

The next day Sandra looked around her homeroom and picked the girl most unlikely to respond. As the bell rang she slid out of her seat and hurried over to Therese, overfed and acne-ed. "Hi," Sandra smiled. That was all, but she meant it.

Later on she caught up with Therese in the cafeteria and sat down next to her. Nobody else in school would do that. Therese was used to eating alone.

Another afternoon she had a Coke with her in the hangout across the street. Then she invited Therese to spend a weekend with her at her house. On Sunday she took her to church . . . and Therese met Jesus.

"When Sandra called me," Jabo said, "she was goin' ape. 'It works! It works! Jabo, it works!'

"And she told me that Therese had spoken out that night in their fellowship group at church. 'I thought there wasn't a single person in that school who cared whether I lived or died—until the day Sandra said hi to me.' And she swallowed and went on softly, 'It might sound Mickey Mouse to you, but I went to the bathroom that morning and cried for two hours.' That's how bad some people are hurting," Jabo added.

A life on a life—the chain goes on. There is no end to this story. The life of God flowing from Leona to Jabo to Sandra to Therese. From Kirk to Milliken to Bobo to hundreds of kids on the city streets.

It's Winston and Carpenter and Kellogg in the Steel City and

Sangster and Chesney in Chicago. And Dr. John Porter pulling more men together in a network of cities—Bowman, Brewster, Daniels, Thompkins.

It's the flesh-and-blood model, no matter what color, what age. It's the action Christ in action. In Columbus, St. Louis, Phoenix, Portland, Billings, Sioux Falls, Peoria, Spokane, Kansas City, Tulsa, Charlotte, Paris, Manila, Seoul. The

Dr. John Porter,
director of urban affairs

hands extend. The smile spreads. The chain lengthens, link by link.

Jesus was a master at touching people, and he still is. But he chooses people today to be the touchers with him. "It was my touch with Bill that made the Gospel clear to me," said Barram in Sacramento. "And we who've been privileged to know relationship are the ones who can provide the touch that frees others."

Incarnate. God fleshed out in people. People who are open to be carriers of His love. God's way to plant new life—forever. Always. Totally. The news is good. You too are loved. It works!